FEBRUARY 2022 EDITION

AN ANTHOLOGY OF ARTICLES

BRILLOPEDIA

Contents

Preface

"Start writing, no matter what. The water does not flow until the faucet is turned on".

-Louis L'Amour

This book is a bouquet of articles contributed by students, professors and academicians. Hundreds of students and professors are contributing their work to Brain Booster Articles, we are here to provide ample information about Law and Contemporary issues. Our aim is to provide a platform for today's generation to express their views and ideas on law and contemporary law.

CHAPTER ONE

JUDICIAL REVIEW UNDER ADMINISTRATIVE ACTIONS

Author: Regamitha Radharaj, B.Com LL.B(hons) from The Tamilnadu Dr. Ambedkar law university, School of excellence in law.

INTRODUCTION

The court constitute a dispute resolving mechanism. The primary objective of the court is to settle dispute and dispense justice between one citizen and another. But this judicial review helps to resolve disputes between the individuals and the state and between the various organs. It is necessary to recognize judicial review as a necessary and basic requirement for the construction up of a novel civilization in order to safeguard rights and liberties.

MEANING OF JUDICIAL REVIEW

Judicial review is reviewed by the judge where the lawfulness of decision or action is correct, or there is no effective means of challenge, judicial review is available.

Article 13 Laws inconsistent with or in derogation of the fundamental rights

Under Article 13(2) The state shall not make any law which takes away or abridges the right conferred by this part and make any law made in contravention of this clause shall, to the extend to the contravention, be void and

Article 368 explains Power to amend the constitution and procedure therefor. Under this article 368(3) Nothing in article 13 shall apply to any amendment made under article, the judicial review in Indian constitution

In Shankari Prasad v UOI where the validity of 1st Constitutional amendment adding Article 31A and 31B was challenged.

The power of judicial review is vested in the Supreme court and high courts under Articles 32 and 226 of the constitution is an integral part and essential feature of the constitution, constituting a part of basic structure.

It is a courts power to review the actions of other branches of government, especially the courts power to invalidate legislative and executive actions as being unconstitutional.

HISTORICAL BACKGROUND OF JUDICIAL REVIEW

Britain

In England the parliament is supreme, they don't give any power to the judiciary to review their acts made by them. Though judiciary has expanded and stated clearly about the principle of strict liability in the case of Ryland vs Fletcher and also manufacturer of the goods owes the duty in Donoghue vs Stevenson

United states of America

Being the colony of Britain, judicial review has somehow evolved in United States of America. They declared that the legislative actions are also under the purview of the judicial review. U.S.A doesn't have any expressed provisions to exercise the power of judicial review. the US landmark case Marbury v Madison (1803) explains the concept of judicial review

India

In the case of Kesavananda Bharati vs State of Kerala Salon as some fundamental rights exist and are a part of the constitution, the power of judicial review has also to be exercised with a view to see that the guarantees afforded by these rights are not contravened, judicial review has thus become an integral part of our Constitutional system.

THREE ASPECTS OF JUDICIAL REVIEW

1. To protect the legality of the essential rights under Part III (Fundamental rights) of the Indian constitution
2. To authorize the neutrality of organizational achievement
3. Interrogation of public interest.

L. Chandra Kumar v. Union of India "that the power of judicial review over legislative action vested in the High Courts under Article 226 and in the Supreme Court under Article 32 of the Constitution is an integral and essential feature of the Constitution, constituting part of its basic structure".

FACET OF JUDICIAL REVIEW IN INDIA

- High court and Supreme Court both applies the judicial review

The concept of Judicial review is used by both the courts under the Article 32 and 226 entrusted in the constitution

- Judicial review for both central and state laws.

The orders, ordinances, rules, constitutional amendments made by the state or centre, judicial review can be constructed.

- A limitations

Judicial review is restricted to the laws incorporated under IX schedule of the constitution. In the IX schedule, out of 284 laws which are protected from judicial review.

- It covers laws and not government issues.

Judicial review applies only to the question of law, it cannot be exercised in respect of political issues. This is also considered as constitutional review. If the court considered the alleged administrative actions is inconsistent, the court will declare it null and void.

- Judicial review is not automatic.

This review can be only used when it has been challenged before the court of law, the Supreme Court does not have the power of judicial review in its own. There is no suo motto power for the supreme court to take cognizance of the action. The power of judicial review will come into place only when it is claimed by the parties to the case.

- Principle of procedure established by law.

The court which it has been challenged should conduct one test, whether the law has been made accordance with procedure established by law, otherwise it would be null and void.

JUDICIAL REVIEW ON ADMINISTRATIVE ACTION

The expression "judicial review" has expanded its reputation since it has exercised it in much different form. Even after the 4TH amendment of the Constitution of India the court had the power to review compensation or the principles for fixing compensation with a view ensuring that it was the just equivalent of the value of property. Since parliament had used the word compensation even after the enactment of fourth amendment. It has no procedural obligations of collecting evidence and weighting argument. It is based on the subjective satisfaction, subjective satisfaction being a condition precedent for the exercise of the power of preventive detention.

It does not mean that administrative authorities are wholly immune by the judicial review, it made by facts of each case.

A.K. Kraipak vs. Union of India

The questions raised where the action of the administrative authority is administrative or quasi judicial in nature, to whom the power is given, the framework within which power is conferred and the consequences.

Issuing directions without the procedure established by law will be a violation and leads to a disciplinary action. The following points will be the grounds for judicial administrative action.

- Illegality:

The court has the power to look into the issues that the public authorities not using their position out of their scope.

- Irrationality:

This ground will help to look into the separation of powers entrusted in the democracy. The misuse of power should not be done by either of the wings of the democracy

- Procedural impropriety:

The procedures entrusted under each wing should be followed by them while executing their duty towards the nation.

- Proportionality.

The separation of powers should be in equal proportion that each wings of the democracy should have the same level of power in the while legislating, executing and making decisions.

CURRENT FRAMEWORK IN INDIA

The government should not interfere in administrative decisions until unless there is a violation in the constitution. The court should not interfere in the policy matters which are within the purview of the government unless it is shown to be contrary to law or inconsistent with the provisions of the constitution. Judicial review is not a matter of exclusion of judicial review but of judicial "Self-restraint".

The functioning of the government is unthinkable without the judicial review entrusted in the constitution. The judiciary power of reviewing is often criticised as judicial overreach which generalization is misguided says Chief justice of India NV Ramana.

CONCLUSION

Judicial review is an important part of the constitution. Even though it has been taken from United Kingdom but creates an impact in the Indian constitution. It does not express defined under constitution but still visible in every page of the constitution. To create more laws and legislate with clarity judicial review is needed.

CHAPTER TWO

MENSTRUAL BENEFIT BILL

Author: Tanisha Maheshwari, I Year of B.A.,LL.B(Hons.) From Christ (Deemed to be University) Delhi NCR.

INTRODUCTION

Menstruation has been an extremely sensitive and troubling topic since time immemorial. We have failed to recognize and take notice of how imperative it is to talk about it. People have always been hesitant and continue to shy away. With each passing year, we have progressed practically in almost every sphere but it's saddening and dejecting to see mankind falling behind in concepts as basic and vital as menstruation. Not just in rural areas but also in progressive societies there is paucity of awareness. We have euphemized the term period with "that time of the month" or " I am down" and continue to view it as derogatory. At the workplace, such issues become a huge conundrum as manifold factors get involved. There's a dearth of basic understanding of how for some women it might be highly excruciating unlike some who undergo trivial changes. Striking out a balance of both personal and public aspects can be very taxing bringing in the need to have a healthy and productive workspace.

BILL

An inching step towards the ongoing need of menstrual awareness can be seen in the form of the "Menstrual benefit Bill" 2017 proposed by Ninong Erin with the aim of removing disparities and allay and addressing menstrual issues at the workplace.

To name a few; Section 4 of the act provides for paid menstrual leave to employed women and leave from school to girl students above class eight. It is an extremely vital and imperative provision. Women will also be entitled to have thirty minutes break twice a day under section 5 of the bill. Section 10 further provides for punishment to anyone who denies women their leaves and entitlements. Such a comprehensive bill is of pressing priority.

CONSTITUTIONAL PERSPECTIVE

Albeit the bill hasn't been passed it is an effective step towards removing gender specific societal stigma Such steps are based on Intelligible differentia (intelligible basis of creating differentiation) and rational nexus (further the concept of equality) since government under article 15 clause (3) is entitled to make special provisions for people which does not act in contradiction to Article 14 of the constitution instead it further the aim of equality. Deliberations and framing of laws cannot be discarded on the grounds of being a gender specific issue. Article 42 of the constitution specifically provides for humane work conditions and maternity leave which hasn't sparked any gender discriminatory conversations or the provisions of reservation for providing disadvantaged sections with level playing field.

INITIATIVE BY ZOMATO another reformist and forward initiative was taken by Zomato by providing women with ten days of paid leaves. It ameliorates the current situation of women who comprise a reasonable proportion of the workforce. Taking into consideration such issues and deviating from norm of identical treatment foster a culture of equality and act as a catalyst for bringing change.

It might come across as a new concept for certain sections of society however there are regions that have been upfront since the very beginning. In the State of Bihar, female government employees have been availing paid leaves since 1992. Kerala is one step further in providing menstrual leave to girls since way back from 1912.

JUDICIARY

The judiciary has been actively addressing the issue. A PIL was filed by Delhi Labour Union seeking paid menstrual leave of four days to all classes of women. It brought into light the reality of the situation and ensuring preservation of fundamental human rights. The court directed the government to take address the PIL in accordance with provisions in the law.

Courts have been fostering inclusivity. Citing Sabrimala case in which menstruating women were barred from entering into the temples and worshipping due to impurity which was direct infringement of right to equality.

CONTRASTING OPINIONS

There are two polarised opinions on this subject matter.

people who are in compliance with it. The basis of creating this difference is intelligible hence it is in furtherance of equality and promotes gender sensitization by coming under the ambit of affirmative action. Being a biological phenomenon, we cannot hold women liable for seeking benefits of such provisions since it is an inevitable process. Symptoms can be highly debilitating and severe for some women, confining to not just cramps but body aches, nausea, headaches, bloating, fatigue, etc. Hence, such provisions become vital to assuage the suffering and create a healthy work environment. Differential treatment becomes important for ensuring access to equality more than hampering it.

on the contrary, some people believe these provisions will result in hesitation and predilection against the female workforce and will have a bleak outcome and exacerbate the already worsen situation. Or some men might object and demand paid leaves for themselves since it is seeming gender-biased. It will go against the notion of inclusivity or hinder the pursuit of equal opportunities. Owing to the biological aspect of this phenomenon it might not be similar for everyone. It will end up with feeling of segregation and alienation. Provisions comes across as generalising and gendering which will ultimately hamper the inclination of companies towards hiring female employees.

<u>CONCLUSION</u>

As progressive citizens its need of the hour and high time to cease the distasteful comments and stigma linked with menstruation. Juxtaposing contemporary scenario with a decade back we have come a far way in terms of progress. Demeaning and belittling people on an ineluctable biological phenomenon shows of the society we come from and it must be eradicated from root level and impacts of entrenched forms of inequality should be minimised.

CHAPTER THREE

LEGISLATIONS ADOPTED BY CHINA TO PROMOTE SPECIAL ECONOMIC ZONES

Author: Shivangi Pathak, IV year of B.A.,LL.B from Faculty of Law, Delhi Metropolitan Education, Affiliated to Guru Gobind Singh Indraprastha University.

<u>WHAT IS THE SPECIAL ECONOMIC ZONES</u>

The liberal meaning of the special economic zones is it set forth the duty-free peninsula for the purpose of the trade operations as well as the duty tariffs which is technically used for overseas territory or we can in another language it is the particular area that sez is certain area where the laws are different from the typically economic law which followed by any country. "The role behind the birth of special economic zones or the need of it is to actually increase foreign investments. They are many countries who adopted the technique of the special economic zones including China, India, Jordan, Russia, Poland, Philippines, Kazakhstan. The profit which its get from the SEZs is they produce goods at the lower price to become globally most competitive countries and control the power against other countries in the world because to increase in the SEZs the benefit also gave them by the help of the trade balance, effective administration, employment, job creation etc".

<u>PURPOSE OF THE SPECIAL ECONOMIC ZONE's</u>

The foremost reason of the establishment of the SEZs in the china is to improve the material life of the Chinese people by the socialistic revolution. Secondly, the root laws for the economic structure surpasses the ideologies of the people and day by day they ere focused to increase the economic conditions by the foreign countries trading rather to make themselves helpless from the previous condition of the china. Among the various countries of the world there are experience which can borrow and also form in the best of it and ultimately their own economic infrastructure. After that, leasing system introduced to raised their own level to overcome the challenges behind them or in front of them. According to the Lenin establishment of the leasing system help the Soviet Union to acquire large enterprises. "All in all, the numerous research work and discussions had made on to the subject matter of the special economic zones and also boil down some considerations. The need of the hour in china is to promote the economic changes as well as the technical changes with the foreign because which involves the payment and exploit the socialist to increase the profit and reduce the cost by that they rule the power in respect of the other countries."

<u>HOW THE SPECIAL ECONOMIC ZONES WORK IN CHINA</u>

The actual zenith of the SEZs is ruling to the advertisement of the technological as well as the economy association which gained enough wideness the course of development. "We witness few stages in the china who are at the pinnacle in the field of zenith. From the starting if we started then there is a particular piece of land of about one square kilometre (Shekou)was specifies out of the Shenzhen which plays the role to export the cooperative projects and also the various joint ventures which was binding between china merchant steam navigation co-foreign firms and Hong Kong Chinese enterprise who are managing the administration of transporting the items, handling the stuff related on the subject of the hiring of labours as well as giving the approvals of the projects and various important things". After that not a year had completed and the news came before them that Guangdong has three SEZs from the help of Shenzhen who were designated for the devolvement over there and also help them in the technology provided from foreign countries to various fields including commerce, culture and agriculture. Since the starting of the SEZs in the china Shenzhen had developed the country to an another level they set forth the high standard against everyone who broadened the concept of the devolvement in the course of SEZs who set specific laws , some material incentives to stable the boosting the energy in the employees as the province separated from the rest of the country also distinct always in the matter of economically and also administratively but the USP of the Shenzhen is that though it is separated from the rest of the country but It will closely connected to the rest of the world.

WHERE ARE THE SPECIAL ECONOMIC ZONES IN THE CHINA

There are the four special economic zones in the china which are located along the cost of the South China and also closely placed with each other. So, they don't face the difficulties to the reach effective administration including port facilities and international trade. These four are Shenzhen, Zhuhai, Hongkong, Macau. The first two shares the borders with other two so they get profit by the established markets for eastern trading ports. The excellent transport and communication service source of invested economy get by only from the Hong Kong. Many foreign ports gave birth are in so far connected to these port cities.

THE LEGISLATION ADOPTED BY CHINA

The laws always used to regulate the discipline between others with fairness so as with the SEZs it helps with the policy package as well as the implements the principles which is pillars for the effective administration of that.

When there is the discussion on the matter of legislations then SEZs has the greater autonomy in their hands. "After being passed by the local PC or PCSC, a SEZ regulation only needs to be submitted to the NPCSC for filing. When a SEZ regulation goes into effect is determined by the local PC or PCSC; the procedure of submitting for filing is purely a matter of notification and does not affect its legal effect". Although the procedures of that legislations is anyway tighter and take ordinarily regulations by relatively a lot.

The reason behind the efficacy of the SEZs rules than the central rules of the china , The main reason is that the SEZs' legislative authority has been confirmed by which indicates that the SEZs' legislative authority has been constitutionally entrenched (the LL is a constitutional law).

During the establishment of the SEZs the leaders gave the concerned to the "special economic zones" the to the "political zones" of the country

The actually economic system from which the country evolve is different from the special economic zones economy system. the rules and regulations which must be followed by the SEZs cities empowers by LL

SHENZEN SPECIAL ECONOMIC ZONE LEGISLATIONS

Market economy is not friendly in the 1980s as well as 1990s. they enhance it only by their hard work and their discipline which by setting the rules and regulations to set forth.as they adopted 19 regulations in the legislations of the SEZs in the Shenzhen. By the means of the contract Shenzhen allowed to Guangdong to recruit their labour force or to dismiss..

When the Shenzhen forwarding in making rules for the SEZs at that time period Shenzen Municipal People Government issues more than 160 Government rules. In 1993 they adopted joint stock company system . to founding the joint stock company loacal administration approval is requied., but under regulations join stock company approval no required.(art. 4).

Legislating for a Market Economy

There are two types of SEZs legislations which provide actual patter of the work for a market economy. They were always introducing rules and regulations on a market economy while others in the world is the under the tree of traditional economy. Local economic development facilitates the policies and regulations in the market economy. National legislation impact by its most effective way is the sanction of the granting land leases which is adopted by Shenzhen in 1987 also with help of the land management law already in the given article 2 and 10 were still play the effective role.

CHAPTER FOUR

PRESENT LEGAL SCENARIO OF RIGHT OF PRIVATE DEFENCE IN INDIA

Author: Khushi Bansal, I year BA.LL.B from Symbiosis Law School, NOIDA.

INTRODUCTION

Every person is entitled to the right to protect himself or herself when there is danger or fear of injury. This right is vested in private defence. Private defence as the word suggests means protection of oneself or of one's property. Defence here implies use of limited force in order to protect oneself from getting hurt. According to the law, limited force can be used and the force used should be reasonable and should be equal to the injury inflicted upon. Though law of torts is uncodified but, the provisions of private defence is given in CHAPTER-IV under Section 96-106 of the Indian

Penal Code,1860.

Illustration for better understanding of this right:

1. X, a thief shows a rod towards T saying that he would kill T if he doesn't handover his volet to him. T, to defend himself snatches the rod from X's hand and hit him hard on his leg. X, though hurt was saved. Will T be liable in this case? T will not be liable in this case as the act done by T was in order to protect his life and movable property (Volet). So, this was an act of private defence on the part of T and will not be liable.
2. B, a 23-year-old girl was returning from her office late night. While she was walking, a man grabbed her from behind and tried to assault her. She hit the man's head with a stone lying on the floor as a result of which the man had several injuries. Here B was not at all liable as this was an act of private defence.

NEED OF THIS RIGHT

1. It is necessary to protect a person or his/her property whether movable or immovable
2. It could also be used to protect one's liberty
3. The law empowers a person to use force when required to save himself/herself from serious injury.

HISTORY OF THE RIGHT OF PRIVATE DEFENCE

This right started with Rome, Italy when in ancient times, there were two defences available for homicide i.e., excusable and justifiable. Private defence was one of the defences under justifiable defences. This was the origin of private defence.

In India, this right was introduced during colonial rule by Lord Macaulay as he was of the opinion that one should always use some amount of force if injury is inflicted upon oneself. Since then, private defence is introduced in Indian Legal System.

The law of private defence has undergone certain changes in England. In ancient England, it was absolute liability of person who protected oneself if something happens while exercising right of private defence. But, in present day England, even homicide committed as a result of private defence is justifiable.

SELF DEFENCE V. PRIVATE DEFENCE

Self-defence and private defence are sometimes used interchangeably but there is a thin line difference between the two. Self-defence means protection of the individual alone or self- protection whereas private defence means protection of oneself or one's property or any other person or any other person's property.

This means that self-defence is only concerned with individual itself whereas private defence is concerned with the individual as well as the protection of other person and also of property. Self-defence is a small circle within a large circle i.e., private defence.

PRESENT LEGAL SCENARIO OF PRIVATE DEFENCE IN INDIA

The right of private defence is given under Chapter-IV of Indian Penal Code, 1860 from Section 96-106. The definition of private defence is not mentioned in the IPC and so it is the discretion of courts to decide which case will come under private defence.

As per Section 96 of Indian Penal Code, no act is an offence which is done under private defence. This means that if a person has used reasonable force to get rid of more serious injury, then it is not an offence. This right, in India is available for oneself and body of other person OR person's property or property of any other person. This property can be both movable as well as immovable property.

A question often arises in our mind that Can we use private defence against a person of unsound mind? The answer is Yes. According to Section 98 of IPC, the right of private defence is available against person of unsound mind, intoxicated person or person with any misconception. For example, A who is intoxicated attempts to kill Z. Z, under his protection hurts A with a rod. Here, Z is not liable as he was only trying to protect himself.

There are some situations where this right is not available. These are:

1. If an act is done by a public servant, then, defence cannot be used because it is believed to be done in good faith. But the act should not be of such a degree which can cause death or excessive hurt to a person.
2. An act directed by public servant
3. A situation where there was time to contact the public authorities.

Some cases of private defence which can even lead to the death of a person which includes assault with apprehension of death, grievous hurt, rape, kidnapping, unnatural lust, wrongful confining a person. Another right was included according to Nirbhaya Act, 2013 where if there is an act of throwing acid, and death of the person throwing it is caused, this will not be considered as an offence. This was the defences against body of a person. There are also provisions against property for which causing death will not be considered as an offence. These include robbery, mischief by fire, trespass, house breaking by night.

According to section 106, this right is also available against deadly assault even to cause harm to innocent person. For example, if there is a mob lynching of 'B' and B, in order to protect himself starts firing on the mob. During the firing an innocent child is hit who got mixed with the mob. In this case, as per Section 106, B will not be liable.

These are the provisions of private defence according to the present legal scenario in India.

CASE ANALYSIS OF NABIA BAI V. STATE OF MADHYA PRADESH, A CASE ON RIGHT OF PRIVATE DEFENCE

Appellant- Nabia Bai

Respondent- State of Madhya Pradesh

Bench- K Singh, R Sahai

FACTS- In this case, the accused Nabia Bai who was also the appellant in Supreme Court was working in the fields along with her mother and sister. All three of them were weeding the crops. The deceased then entered the field with a knife and attacked them. When this tussle was going on, Nabia Bai got hold of the knife and inflicted several cuts on the deceased which led to the death.

JUDGEMENT PRONOUNCED BY SC – The court held that Nabia Bai had neither intention nor motive to kill the person who attacked her family in fields. She wanted to protect herself, her mother and her sister from getting injured via knife. The judgement of the lower court which sentenced Nabia Bai to seven years of imprisonment was struck down by the Supreme Court and she was acquitted.

This was a judgement where right of defending oneself and other persons was upheld though it led to the death of the attacker. Still, Nabia Bai was acquitted by the apex court since her act was done in good faith.

CONCLUSION

After doing all the research we can conclude that one can use only reasonable force in order to defend oneself. The force used should match with the injury inflicted upon. The right to private defence is given from section 96 to 106 of the Indian Penal Code. There are several exceptions to this right and certain situation where even if death is occurred, no offence will be considered. We also saw the case of Nabia Bai where the force used led to the death of the person but the accused was acquitted since there was no intention to kill the person. One should use private defence as a shield, not a sword.

Ronald Regal, 40th US President has rightly said. "Self-defence is not only our right; it is a duty."

CHAPTER FIVE

WHY INDIA NEED TO BE VOCAL FOR LOCAL?

Author: Suchita Garg, I Year of LLM (Criminal and Security Laws) from Sabarmati University.

<u>Abstract</u>

By being vocal for local, we aren't eliminating globalisation, but calling for a new form of it. Self-reliance in the new vision for the country and it is neither exclusionary nor isolationist. Local has helped us through this crisis and has helped us stay alive. By improving our local business and productive efficiency, we can compete with the world as well as help the world.

There needs to be more focus on supporting local products. Home-grown products shouldn't just be bought but also actively promoted and marketed. We need to encourage local business to improve supply chains across the country and boost the economy. When Prime Minister Narendra Modi addressed the nation, he spoke about the strengths of the nation when it comes to stepping up in times of difficult phrase.

<u>Introduction</u>

Vocal for Local has become the most trending motto which has emerged during the COVID-19 pandemic. However, the knowledge behind this movement is not new. It finds its origins in the Swadeshi movement which was popularised in 1905 during the Indian independence struggle. Developed and encouraged by Mahatma Gandhi and the other great freedom fighters, Swadeshi was conceived as a way to absorb nationalism and nationalistic pride among Indians.

The coronavirus pandemic taught that we need to make sure we can meet our own demand for products. With nations closing down their borders and consolidating inventories, the movement of goods and services across the world came to a virtual halt. Nations were struggling to meet their basic necessities and to substitute for products which are generally imported from other nations.

Global integration is, of course, creditable. So is the idea behind the division of labour and the specialisation in various products and parts of the production process. But it is equally, if not more, significant to be able to satisfy the basic demands for necessities. It took a pandemic to show us the faults in this seemingly perfect structure. It is also important to have substitutes in place so as to not have to struggle in panic as global supply chains break down.

Vocal for local gives clear importance to the domestic industries and the small-scale Kirana stores. In a time where we were struggling to maintain liquidity and regular cash flow, the vocal for local movement can also be seen as an impulse to reawaken demand and hence, to throw a lifeline to the minor and marginal local industries which were struggling to persist in the wake of the pandemic.

Necessity is the mother of invention. Or over here, scarcity is the mother of invention. In times like, when jobs are hard to come by, it is important to adapt to the crunch by creating new jobs through new innovative ideas. This could mean finally setting up, own dream business via an online marketplace, starting an online consulting business to help people in remote areas or any other great business idea on your mind! With incredible software solutions being developed, the opportunities are limitless!

The advantage is three-fold. First, it will decrease dependence on foreign products, and hence, cut down on the import pressure. Second, it will give a fighting chance to inland companies to survive through the crisis period. Third, it will fit in with the monetary backlash against China, and place India in a strategic position to emerge as the new manufacturing centre of the world.

For an economically independent nation, people need to rise to the occasion and support domestic businesses. People need to create products and services that are made in India, made for India and also made for the world. People also need to refocus our strategies from being profit-driven to becoming more people-centric.

Why the growth of India stopped?

During the Swadeshi movement, when nationalism was in trend, domestic and indigenous industries developed a great deal. However, liberalisation arose in the early 1990s, Swadeshi took a backseat, and Foreign Direct Investment stole the show. With the inflow of external capital and portfolio investments, the Indian markets soon got flooded with an excess of options. Be it goods or services, the products were of better quality and priced more competitively. Local firms were miserably outclassed and gradually faded into oblivion.

The primary reason for this was the presence of excessive bureaucracy and red-tapism. During the 1990s and 2000s, the Indian economy was characterised by the severe bureaucratic control. Since then, however, bureaucratic control has been gradually reduced and industries have been allowed more independence to make their own decisions.

Another reason was the lack of funding options. This was the secondly cause behind the late bloom of the Indian start-up ecosystem. With the relaxation of controls, a number of private equity and venture capital firms have come up, both internal and external. The effect of this can be seen in the increase in the number of Indian start-ups over the last decade. Companies like OYO, Zomato, Paytm and others took full advantage of the easy availability of investors and funding in the Indian economy.

The vocal for local movement or the quest to be self-sufficient

The idea is to promote domestic industries and consume local wherever possible so that the long term effects of an increase in demand can be used to develop the domestic industries and make them self-reliant. This will help in the scale-up of production, and will, make India a manufacturing centre for the world.

At present, some of the sectors are completely dependent on the import of strategic raw materials from different countries, while others are moderately or less dependent.

According to a report published by the Confederation of Indian Industry, 88% of the components used to manufacture cell phones are imported from China. Similarly, the pharmaceutical and medical industry is also dependent on imports, both for medical equipment and medicines. 60% of medical devices are imported, along with raw materials for the manufacture of antibiotics, vitamins and other drugs. The reason why these products are imported from overseas and are not manufactured in India itself is that the manufacture of these raw materials requires large sources of clean water, energy and infrastructural investment. Not only is it economical, but also easy access to better quality products. Then, all Indian firms need to be concern about is the assembling of the final product. It is also because of these reasons why it is challenging for India to reduce its dependency on foreign imports and produce domestic substitutes.

Make in India movement

The manufacturing sector in India has to be developed in such a way that it can provide improved and more competitive prices than the other contenders like Vietnam, Malaysia; etc. The Vocal for Local movement is not the first initiative to make nation a manufacturing hub. It is simply the Make in India movement in a novel avatar.

The Make in India movement was launched in 2014 to give a push to manufacturing firms in India, and with the vision of replacing China as the manufacturing centre. Since its launch, the share of the manufacturing sector in the GDP actually fell instead of rising. This was due to a combination of factors firstly improper policy implementation along with unreasonable ambitions. Secondly, vocal for Local can only be successful if it learns from the mistakes in the Make in India campaign, and adjusts its ambitions and policy implementations accordingly.

Conclusion

The Vocal for Local movement has by now succeeded in its first intention of rising nationalism and the preference to use domestically manufactured items. For prompting export: first is to scale up domestic production, and second is to take up strategic promotion in the targeted nations to build up a market for the products.

Among the list of potential products are textiles, apparels, drugs, furniture etc. To boost local manufacturing, Confederation of Indian Industry suggests measures such as investment in infrastructure, improved port connectivity, specialised initiatives to help people skill-up as well as incentives to promote greater adoption of technology and innovation.

The Fast-Moving Consumer Goods sector is emerging as the poster child for this movement. With companies like Amul, Dabur, Patanjali and Nestle performing at excellent levels, there is simply no need to look beyond borders. The textile and handicrafts sectors are all producing superior products locally. As for India's service sector, like software, IT and banking services, India is already at par, if not superior, in comparison to the peers. Even the Indian pharmaceutical sector has developed as a global leader during the coronavirus pandemic.

The difficulties lie with the core manufacturing sectors, such as electronic equipment, automobile parts, solar equipment and other components. To develop these sectors, it requires strategic policy implementation as well as infrastructural investment.

Apart from these, to make sure that the Vocal for Local movement does not lose steam after the coronavirus pandemic ends, it also requires specific guidelines and initiatives from the government. But this movement needs to be constant for the long-term. Only time will tell whether India succeeds to replace China as the manufacturing centre of the world?

Author's Biography

Suchita Garg is a student in Sabarmati University. She is pursing LLM degree in Criminal and Security laws. She worked hard as an intern at various courts of India. She likes to write about the current happenings around her. The author wrote on this topic because she wants that readers should understand that globalisation is not a bad thing but self- reliance should be the new vision for the county like India. One of the best steps which readers can take is to encourage the local business to boost the economy of the country.

CHAPTER SIX

A CRITICAL APPRAISAL ON THE POWERS AND FUNCTIONS OF LOKPAL AND LOKAYUKTA IN INDIA

Author: khushi Sehgal, III year of B.B.A.,LL.B(Hons.) From Bennett University Greater Noida.

Co-author: Subhangi Das, III year of B.B.A.,LL.B(Hons.) From Bennett University Greater Noida.

Without strong watchdog institutions, impunity becomes the very foundation upon which systems of corruption are built. And if impunity is not demolished, all efforts to bring an end to corruption are in vain.

ABSTRACT

Corruption is a big concern, shown through the well-versed facts alongside various previous physically present evidences provides that endangering the nation's security and stability; threatening socio - economic and political progress; and undermining democratic and moral ideals. Moreover, studies show that corruption is among the chief factors for a lack of economic development and progress in emerging countries as India. Corruption is perceived to get a cumulative impact on investment—both internal and external environment further slows a country's infrastructure. Transformation of current frameworks and changes in transparency standards for public funds expenditure are also part of these demands. The trend of corruption has become one of the primary contributors of the government's delayed pace in executing grandiose projects and programmes, resulting in massive financial losses to the exchequer. Corruption has grown pervasive, with corrupt activities permeating all sectors of the business, government, and society. As a result, India's First Administrative Reforms Commission (ARC) suggested the establishment of two special bodies known as "Lokpal" and "Lokayukta" for the redress of grievances of citizens in 1966. At that time, Dr. LM Singvi firstly coined the concept of Lokpal related to the Ombudsman concept which were followed by many foreign countries like Finland, Denmark, Sweden etc. The Lokpal and Lokayukta Act, 2013 was passed by the Parliament of India which established the statutory body of Lokpal and Lokayukta. The Lokpal was made to fight the corruption in the Union Government whereas the Lokayukta was made for the State Government. In this paper, we shall provide with a critical appraisal on the powers and function of the Lokpal and Lokayukta in India.

INTRODUCTION

"Corruption is just another type of tyranny," said by Joe Bidden, America's 47th Vice President. According to the statement, corruption is on par with cruel and tyrannical government rule. Corruption, on the other hand, is a struggle that a common man or woman encounters every day in order to maintain his or her fundamental rights and other benefits as human beings granted by the Constitution. The growing trends of Corruption in India is a bigger issue which affects the Central, State and the Local Government. According to a study by Transparency International in 2005, it was found that more than 62% of the people has to give bribe to the public officials to make their work done. Thus, this is affecting the country's economy and investments. So, to come up from such situation, India established their first Ombudsman concept which is known as Lokpal and Lokayukta by Administrative Reform Committee in 1966. The statutory body of Lokpal and Lokayukta was mainly made to prevent corruption practices in the country.

In this paper, we will deal with the concept of the statutory bodies called Lokpal and Lokayukta, their origin and history, different acts like Lokpal Bill and Lokpal and Lokayukta Act of 2013, functions and powers of both the bodies and various other concepts.

HISTORY AND ORIGIN OF LOKPAL AND LOKAYUKTA

The concept of Lokpal and Lokayukta was not there in India in the beginning. But the concept of Ombudsman was first instituted in Sweden in 1809. This concept is same as of Lokpal and Lokayukta in India. After second world war, the Ombudsman concept was followed by many foreign countries like in Finland (from 1919), Denmark (from 1953), New Zealand (from 1962) and then in India. The concept of Ombudsman in India first was introduced in 1964 by the Santnama Committee through Central Vigilance Commission (CVC). During that time, Central Vigilance Commission (CVC) was the highest authority for complaints related to corruption matters. It was an independent commission which was working without any interventions of the government. Then, in 1966, first Administrative Reform Committee (ARC) was set up, which was chaired by Morari Dasia. The Committee recommended in its report the establishment of a two-tier monitoring bodies, with a Lokpal at the Central level and Lokayukta at the State level. After recommendation by the Committee in 1968, first Lokpal Bill was introduced in Lok Sabha but it was not passed in Rajya Sabha. The Lokpal Bill was passed eight times in Lok Sabha till 2011 but it was still not passed by Rajya Sabha. Before that, in 2002, Second Administrative Reform Committee was formed that was chaired by MN Venkatachaliah which was made to review the functioning of the Constitution and recommended the appointment of Lokpal and Lokayukta. The committee also stated that Prime Minister ought to be kept out of the ambit of the Lokpal. In 2005, third Administrative Reform Committee was formed which was chaired by Veerappa Moily. Both the committees gave their recommendation to form Lokpal and Lokayukta but it was not listened by the government.

In 2011, Anna Hazare started the movement "India against Corruption" and then finally the Lokpal Bill was passed in both the houses in 2013.

Finally, the bill received assent from President on 1st January 2014 and came into force on 16th January 2014 under the name "The Lokpal and Lokayukta Act 2013".

LOKPAL & ITS STRUCTURE

The word 'Lokpal' is derived from a Sanskrit word 'Lokapala' which means defender of people or people's friend. The Lokpal is an anti – corruption authority or a statutory body who represents public interest in India. It is a form of Ombudsman concept which was taken from foreign countries in 1966. Lokpal is a form of statutory body which is made to solve the issues of corruption on the Central Level. As of 2022, the current chairman of Lokpal in India is Justice Pinaki Chandra Ghose.

Structure of Lokpal

- Lokpal is a statutory body which consists of one chairperson and 8 members in the committee. The Head of the Lokpal or the Chairperson of the Lokpal can be (1) the Chief Justice of India or (2) the former judge of Supreme Court of India or (3) an eminent person who has outstanding ability to possess special knowledge with minimum 25 years of experience in the field related to Anti – corruption policy, public administration, vigilance, finance, law and management.
- The 8 other members of the committee must include 4 judicial members and 4 non – judicial members. Also, 50% of the members of the committee must be from OBC/SC/ST background and women.
- The 4 Judicial members of the committee must be the former judge of Supreme Court of India or the former judge of High Court.
- The 4 non – judicial members of the committee can be a eminent person who has outstanding ability to possess special knowledge with minimum 25 years of experience in the field related to Anti – corruption policy, public administration, vigilance, finance, law and management.

The Term and Appointment in the office of Lokpal

- It should be clearly noted that all the 8 members of the committee will be selected by the Selection Commission of Lokpal which includes 5 members.
- The chairperson and the members of Lokpal is appointed by the President of India on the recommendations of the Selection Commission.

- The members of Selection Commission include: (1) The Prime Minister of India, (2) The Speaker of Lok Sabha, (3) The Leader of Opposition in Lok Sabha, (4) The Chief Justice of India or any Judge nominated by Chief Justice of India, (5) One eminent jurist.
- The chairperson or the head of the Selection Committee is the Prime Minister of the country.
- The term of chairperson and the members of the committee is for 5 years or till the age of 70 years.

POWERS AND FUNCTIONS OF LOKPAL

There are various powers that Lokpal has which includes the following:

- Lokpal has the authority to seize any official's assets, revenues, receipts, or perks obtained via corruption.
- The Lokpal has the authority to propose the removal or suspension of government workers accused of corruption.
- Lokpal has the authority to issue orders to prevent records from being destroyed during the preliminary investigation.
- It has supervisory and directive powers over the CBI (Central Bureau of Investigation), as well as several measures aimed at strengthening the CBI.
- In certain circumstances, the Lokpal's wing has been granted civil court-like powers.
- In the absence of the Government or a competent authority, the Lokpal has the jurisdiction to provide sanction for prosecution of public officers.

The Lokpal also has various functions to perform which includes the following:

- The Lokpal keeps a close eye on all government personnel and can take appropriate action against them if they do not follow the law.
- It can act either on the basis of a private person's complaint or on its own initiative (i.e., on his own initiative). Even before an investigation body (such as the Central Vigilance Commission or the CBI) has launched an investigation, the Lokpal can call or question any public employee if there is a prima facie case against them.
- It can also suggest that his discoveries be put into action.

- For appeals arising out of any other statute currently in force, the Lokpal will serve as the appellate authority.
- Any action made in good faith by a public servant or other official must be protected. It must provide enough protection to individuals who are exploited because they speak out against corruption.

JURISDICTION OF LOKPAL

Jurisdiction of Lokpal includes the following:

- Prime Minister, Ministers, Members of Parliament, Officers from Groups A, B, C, and D, and Central Government Officials.

The jurisdiction of Lokpal extends to the Prime Minister, with the exception of allegations of corruption involving:

- International Relations
- Security
- Public Order
- Atomic energy and Space exploration.

The jurisdiction of the Lokpal does not include ministers and members of Parliament in the matter relating to:

- Any speeches delivered in the Parliament
- For a vote cast in the Parliament.
- The jurisdiction of Lokpal also includes:

Anyone in charge (director/manager/secretary) of a body or society established by a central government act, any society or body supported or controlled by the central government, and anyone involved in abetting, bribe providing, or bribe taking.

LOKAYUKTA AND IT'S ORGANISATIONAL STRUCTURE

Lokayuktas are constrained by statutory provisions in the given state level; their capabilities vary as per the individuality granted to them by these laws, as well as the relationship that exists with the state legislature, which is frequently in a position to impede the efficient implementation of Lokayuktas, as the latter rely on them for assistance in the enforcement of orders, directives, and so on. This scenario has frequently tends to result in the department getting reduced to just a retirement home for former bureaucrats with hardly any power; nevertheless, in some of these states, the establishment has been incredibly efficient and effective, thanks to the shortage of reliance on the state government for assistance in imposing power. According to the current evidences that are the documentation, the proposal for the appointment of Lokayuktas at the state level was developed to increase the standards of public administration by investigating complaints against administrative actions, including cases of corruption, partiality, and official lack of discipline in state bureaucracy. The Lokayukta is established as a statutory authority with a definite term for Woking independently and impartially. The person chosen is generally a former Chief Justice of the High Court or a former Supreme Court judge. Citizens can contact the Lokayukta directly with charges of corruption, nepotism, or any other sort of misuse of power against any government official.

The construction of the Lokayukta does not follow a consistent pattern throughout all states. Certain states, such as Rajasthan, Karnataka, Andhra Pradesh, and Maharashtra, established both the Lokayukta and the Up-Lokayukta, but others, such as Uttar Pradesh and Himachal Pradesh, established just the Lokayukta. The organisation in Madhya Pradesh is organised into four functional branches to support both Lokayukta and the Up-Lokayukta. The first component is the Administrative and Enquiry Section, which is led by the Secretary, who is a senior IAS official who serves as the department's Head of Department for the whole organisation. Then, officials of a rank of District Judge are placed as Legal Advisors to help the Lokayukta and the Up-Lokayukta in dealing with legal concerns and conducting investigations, and an officer of the position of Chief Judicial Magistrate is assigned as Dy. Legal Advisor. Special Police Establishment, which includes the investigation of certain offences affecting public administration and those falling under the terms of the Prevention of Corruption Act, which would be a Central Act.

The Technical Cell handles technical concerns. It is led by the Chief Engineer, with Executive Engineers, Assistant Engineers, and Technical Assistants reporting to him. District Vigilance Committees were Madhya Pradesh's seven Divisional Committees that investigate complaints presented to them by the Lokayukta or the Up-Lokayukta and give a recommendation to the competent authorities. The Lokayukta and Up-Lokayukta are two independent and impartial committees established to probe the actions and decisions of public workers. These authority, which are independent of the legislature and government, are held to the same criteria as Supreme Court and High Court justices. They are appointed by the Governor. When appointing appointments, the Governor confers with the Chief Justice of the State High Court and the Leader of the Opposition in the State Legislative Assembly.

Lokpal is indeed a cross body with one chairperson and a maximum of eight members. Half of the utmost eight members shall be judicial members, and at least half of the rest will be from the SC/ ST/ OBC/ Minorities and women. A judicial member of the Lokpal must be a former Supreme Court Judge or a former Chief Justice of a High Court. The tenure of service for the Lokpal Chairman and Members is 5 years, or until they reach the age of 70. The Lokpal Act of 2013 requires the DoPT to compile a list of candidates interested in serving as chairman or members of the Lokpal. This list will now be forwarded to the planned eight-member search committee, which would shortlist individuals and present them to the Prime Minister-led selection panel. The search committee's choices or may not be chosen by the selection panel.

The government formed a search committee in September 2018, led by former Supreme Court Justice Ranjana Prakash Desai. The 2013 Act further mandates that all states establish the Lokayukta department within one year of Act's implementation. The Selection Panel may establish its own systematic method for selecting the Chairperson and Members of the Lokayukta.

<u>JURISDICTION</u>

In the Lokayuktas jurisdiction there is no consistency. As an example, In Himachal Pradesh, Andhra Pradesh, Madhya Pradesh, and Gujarat, the State Government is subject to Lokayukta's purview, however in Maharashtra, Uttar Pradesh, Rajasthan, and Bihar, he or she is not. The Lokayukta has authority over ministers and higher-ranking government officials in the majority of states. Maharashtra has also featured former politicians and public servants. Lokayukta has jurisdiction over members of state legislatures in Andhra Pradesh, Himachal Pradesh, Gujarat, and Uttar Pradesh. The Lokayukta is accountable to the state legislature. Its yearly report is presented in the legislature, and its recommendations are often adopted either by houses.

<u>LOKAYUKTA – POWERS AND FUNCTIONS</u>
POWER

The Lokayukta supports those in bringing corruption to light, primarily among politicians and government employees. In provinces like as Himachal Pradesh, Andhra Pradesh, Madhya Pradesh, and Gujarat, the chief minister is subject to Lokayukta's supervision, however in Orissa, Bihar, Rajasthan, Uttar Pradesh, and Maharashtra, he is not.

In practically all states, ministers and higher-ranking public workers are also subject to the Lokayukta's jurisdiction. It is worth noting that the Lokayukta conducts raids but has no binding authority to punish anybody, merely recommending punishment to the government.

This has the authority to conduct raids on the homes and offices of corrupt officials at the state level, as well as to request pertinent files and documents from state government agencies. It also has the authority to examine and visit public authorities that are under investigation.

The Lokayukta may examine any action committed by a public servant whether it is reported by the state government. However, the Lokayukta has the ability to advise punishment it against perpetrator to the administration, but it is up to the state to accept or change the ideas.

FUNCTIONS

Assessing "concerns" of citizens triggered by gross incompetence, misuse of authority, and lack of integrity against state-level public employees, and recommending action once proven. The Lokayukta is responsible with resolving public grievances against politicians and government employees as quickly as possible.

The Lokayukta and Uplokayukta will furnish the Governor of the state with a summary report on their activities. As a result, they are accountable to the state legislature. Its second critical purpose is to keep anti-corruption agencies and authorities accountable for their investigations. By enlisting the services of a special investigating officer, it conducts fair and unbiased inquiries based on facts against the accused individual.

A comprehensive yearly report on the execution of their tasks shall be provided to the Governor, and an important concern about the power of the Lokayukta was raised under the Bangalore Lokayukta Act, 1984. In a landmark case, the High Court ruled that even if the Lokayukta is required to examine a grievance against a public worker other than the Chief Minister, a member of the state legislature, or a secretary, he however has no jurisdiction unless granted by a notice issued by the state authority. Under the rules of the Act, the Lokayukta has no jurisdiction to investigate a complaint against the vice-chancellor since the authority is prohibited by

Section 14 of the Universities Grants Commission Act, 1956.

CRITICISM OF THE EXISTING LOKPAL AND LOKAYUTKA SET

Establishments that pursue the framework of an Ombudsman are a requisite which need to be developed nowadays age to check the power and authority that is given to the Management, but while institutions such as the Lokayukta are developed political pressure, the Executive goes to great lengths to make it a hollow organisation, with no actual authority. This happens in two ways: either the government ensures that the framework itself is so weak that the Ombudsman has no real authority, or it controls the nomination of the Ombudsman in a very manner that a malleable individual is chosen, and their advice are not counted. Similarly, the Lokpal body has attempted to bring about the most reform in the fight against corruption in India's administrative system, but there are gaps and inconstancies that must be addressed.

Five years went since parliament enacted the Lokpal and Lokayuktas Act 2013, yet not a single Lokpal has been appointed, demonstrating a lack of political will. The Lokpal Act also required states to appoint a Lokayukta within a year of its enactment. However, the Lokayukta has been constituted in just 16 states.

Board is not immune to political influence because the hiring committee is made up of representatives of political parties. The Act of 2013 did not provide specific immunity to informants and possibility for launching an investigation against the complaint if the accused is determined to be innocent would only dissuade individuals from filing complaints. The most significant gap is the absence of the judiciary from the Lokpal's purview. There is no constitutional support for the Lokpal, and there is no effective framework for appeals against the Lokpal. The specifics of the selection of the Lokayukta have been left entirely up to the states.

CONCLUSION

A really renowned individual once remarked that the most magnificent work of God is an honest person. When men are clean, laws are pointless; when they are corrupt, laws are null and void. Political corruption thrive in society as people tolerate them without protest. Notably, the three pillars of democracy (Legislative, Executive, and Judiciary) must be well-organized, free of corruption, and free of defects in operation. It is crucial to acknowledge that the current institutional framework is grossly insufficient to address issues of corruption and governance failure. The present Lokpal and Lokayukta institutions have too little independence, and future legislation is pointless unless the issue of executive influence over these organisations is resolved. However, because the Lokayukta system in India is not standard and differs state vice and have indeed been deprived their mechanism of investigation with their right of autonomy. To combat corruption, the institution of the ombudsman should be enhanced in terms of the functional independence as well as personnel allocation. Greater openness, greater access to information, and citizen and citizen group empowerment are essential, as well as competent leadership prepared to expose itself to public criticism.

Authors' Biography

I Khushi Sehgal and Subhangi Das are 3rd year students of Bennett University, Greater Noida, pursuing BBA LLB (Hons.). We had a keen interest in Administrative Law which made us do more research work on the interesting topics which are covered under the purview of this law. Administrative Law is a wide area of law which deals with various aspects such as: Judicial Control, Publication of rules, delegation of powers and many more. Through our research, we have attempted to write about the powers and functions of Lokayukta and Lokpal in India in a simpler form.

CHAPTER SEVEN

APPLICABILITY OF CENTRAL LAWS IN J&k AFTER ABROGATION OF ARTICLE 370

Author: Arnav Sharma, III Year of B.A.,LL.B(Hons.) From Chandigarh University.

Applicability of central laws in Jammu and Kashmir after abrogation of Article 370 . Firstly, it is important to know the background about what article 370 was so the Article 370 of Indian constitution gave the special status to state of Jammu and Kashmir which was administered from 1954

to 31 October 2019 conferring it with the power to have a separate constitution, a state flag autonomy over internal administration of the state. constitution. Article 370 was drafted in Part XXI of the Indian constitution titled "Temporary, Transitional and Special Provisions given special rights and live under separate set of laws including laws related to citizenship, ownership of property and fundamental rights. Before abrogation of article 370 the Jammu and Kashmir follows their own always there were different laws which are followed in Jammu and Kashmir for example in whole India the Indian penal code is Applicable whereas in Jammu and Kashmir RPC is applicable which is Ranbir penal code after abrogation of article all the acts made by centre are extended to the UT of Jammu and Kashmir.

As Kashmir was a issue from years that's why government decided to make the state as union territory after abrogation government made two union territories one is Jammu & Kashmir and second is Ladakh. The both the union territories share common high court called Jammu and Kashmir and Ladakh High Court. In addition, after abrogation of article 370 the reorganisation act 2019 came in existence which was passed by the parliament enacting the division of state of Jammu and Kashmir into two union territory mainly Jammu and Kashmir and Ladakh.

After abrogation of article 370 many laws were implemented as many as 106 central laws were enacted by centre & 164 state laws were reappealed The most important among the 106 Central Laws which will become applicable to both the Union Territories are the Code of Civil Procedure, 1908; the Code of Criminal Procedure, 1973; the Indian Penal Code, 1860; the Aadhar (Targeted Delivery of Financial and Other Subsidies, Benefits and Services) Act, 2016; the Administrative Tribunal Act, 1985; the Anand Marriage Act, 1951; the National Commission for Minority Education Institutions Act, 2005; the National Commission for Teacher Education Act, 1993; the Arbitration and Conciliation Act, 1996, the Benami Transactions (Prohibition) Act, 1988, the Commercial Courts Act, 2015; the Commission for Protection of Child's Rights Act, 2006; the Disturbed Area (Special Courts) Act, 1976; the Dowry Prohibition Act, 1961; the Drugs and Magic Remedies (Objectionable Advertisement) Act, 1954; the Energy Conservation Act, 2001; the Enemy Property Act, 1968; the Family Courts Act, 1984; the Gram Nyalayas Act, 2009; the Hindu Succession Act, 1956; the Juvenile Justice (Care and Protection of Children) Act, 2015; the Maintenance and Welfare of Parents and Senior Citizens Act, 2007; the Muslim Personal Law (Shariat) Application Act, 1937, the Muslim Women

(Protection of Rights on Divorce) Act, 1986 and the National Commission for Minorities Act, 1992.

The other important Central Laws are the National Commission for Women Act, 1990; the Prevention of Corruption Act, 1988; the Prevention of Damage to Public Property Act, 1984; the Protection of Children from Sexual Offences Act, 2012; the Prohibition of Child Marriage Act, 2007; the Protection of Human Rights Act, 1994; the Protection of Women from Domestic Violence Act, 2005 and the Right to Information Act, 2005 etc. The acts which are reappealed were Among the State Laws which are going to be repealed in the Union Territory of Jammu and Kashmir and Union Territory of Ladakh are J&K Accountability Commission Act, 2002; J&K Arya Samajist Marriages (Validation) Act, 1942; Buddhists Polyandrous Marriages Prohibition Act, 1941; Jammu and Kashmir Charitable Endowments Act, 1989; J&K Cinematograph Act, 1933; Code of Civil Procedure Samvat 1977; Code of Criminal Procedure, Samvat 1989; J&K State Commission for Women Act, 1999; J&K Consumer Protection Act, 1987; J&K Criminal Law Amendment Act, 1993; J&K Delhi Adalat's Act,2013; J&K Displaced Persons (Permanent Settlement) Act, 1971; J&K Dissolution of Muslim Marriages Act, 1942; J&K Electricity Act, 2010; J&K State Evacuees (Administration of Property and Validation of Orders, Proceedings) Act, 1958.

The other State Laws, which are going to become thing of past, included J&K Evidence Act Samvat 1977; J&K Forest Act, Samvat 1987; J&K Juvenile Justice (Care and Protection of Children) Act, 2013; J&K Muslim Specified Wakafs and Special Properties (Management and Regulation) Act, 2004; J&K Prevention of Corruption Act, Samvat 2006; J&K Permanent Residents Certificate (Procedure) Act, 1963; J&K Prevention of Illicit Traffic in Narcotic Drugs and Psychotropic Substances Act, 1988; , State Ranbir Penal Code, Samvat 1989; J&K Right to Information Act, 2009; J&K Transfer of Property Act, 1977 and J&K Wakafs Act, 2001 etc.

The Governor's Acts, which are not going to be applicable in the Union Territory of Jammu and Kashmir and Union Territory of Ladakh, are J&K Real Estate (Regulation and Development) Act, 2018; J&K State Commission for Protection of Women and Child Rights Act, 2018; J&K Prohibition of Benami Property Transactions Act, 2018; J&K Rights of Persons with Disabilities Act, 2018; J&K Family Courts Act, 2018; J&K Commercial Courts Act, 2018; J&K State Trust for Welfare of Persons with Autism Cerebral Palsy, Mental Retardation and Multiple Disabilities Act,

2018; J&K Single Window (Industrial Investment and Business Facilitation) Act, 2018 and J&K Drugs and Magic Remedies (Objectionable Advertisements) Act, 2018 etc.

The State Laws which shall be applicable to the Union Territory of Jammu and Kashmir and Union Territory of Ladakh with amendments are Transfer of Property Act; J&K Alienation of Land Act; the Jammu and Kashmir Big Landed Estates Abolition Act; the J&K Land Grants Act; the J&K Agrarian Reforms Act; the J&K Cooperative Societies Act and the J&K Reservation Act.

A total of 166 other State Acts including Governor's Acts will remain in force in both the Union Territories as these laws were enacted by the State Legislature from time to time keeping in view State specific requirements and these will have importance even after bifurcation of the State.

Some Important laws which are now applicable UT of Jammu and Kashmir mentioned below: -

Civil Procedure Code (CPC): - The Civil Procedure code regulates every action in civil courts. The aim of the procedural law is to implement the substantive law. This code ensures fair justice by enforcing the rights and liabilities. This was not there before revocation of article 370 this is now extended to union territory of Jammu and Kashmir before abrogation the state has separate laws.

Code of Criminal Procedure (CrPC): - The Code of Criminal Procedure is the main legislation on procedure for administration of substantive criminal law in India. This code is now Applicable in UT of Jammu and Kashmir.

Indian Penal Code (IPC): - The Indian Penal code (IPC) is the official criminal code of India. It is comprehensive code intended to cover all substantive aspects of criminal law before abrogation the Ranbir penal code (RPC) followed in state of Jammu and Kashmir.

Arbitration and conciliation: - It is an act that regulates domestic arbitration in India. It was amended in 2015 and further amendment was passed in 2019 it extends to UT of Jammu and Kashmir. Before abrogation of article 370 the act was called the act of Jammu and Kashmir arbitration and conciliation act 1997.

Limitation Act: - The limitation act provides the time limit for different suits within, which an aggrieved person can approach the court for redress or justice. It is now extended to the Union Territory of Jammu and Kashmir Before abrogation of article 370 the state of Jammu and Kashmir has different limitation act namely Jammu and Kashmir limitation act.

<u>Conclusion</u>

After researching the topic I would like to conclude that it is essential to abrogate article 370 because this will lead Government to implement the laws freely because when article 370 was there the laws were to be passed separately In Jammu and Kashmir legislature then they are implemented I think there should one nation law system there should be no such provision in which the laws to be passed separately by states there should be only one type of the law which is applicable in whole of India previously before abrogation of article 370 any law passed by central government is not applicable to state of Jammu and Kashmir after abrogation of article 370 every law is extended to the union territory of Jammu and Kashmir. Many changes took place like new land reform came in existence like before the article was abolished only people residing in the state are allowed to buy the land but after abrogation

Article 370 the new reforms came in existence now everyone can do the investments or buy land if they fulfil certain criteria prescribed by government. As per me it is necessary to have central laws implemented as compare to separate laws of Jammu and Kashmir to maintain transparency in the system and for smooth functioning.

CHAPTER EIGHT

GIRL CHILD KILLED IN WOMB

Author: Kumari Muskan, II Year of B.A.,LL B from Sai Nath University.

<u>INTRODUCTION</u>

Infanticide in India has a history that lasts for centuries. Poverty, the lending system, the birth of unmarried women, infants with disabilities, starvation, lack of support services and birth defects such as postpartum depression are some of the factors suggested to explain the prevalence of female genital mutilation in India.

Although infanticide has become a crime in India, it is still a relatively low crime rate due to a lack of reliable data. In 2010, the National Crime

Records Bureau reported nearly 100 infant and female infanticide, producing a legal rate of less than one million child murders per million.

The Indian practice of female genital mutilation (FGM) and gender-based abortions have been cited to partially describe gender inequality reported as increasingly perverted since the 1991 Census of India, although there may be other factors that may contribute to this practice.

DEFINITION

Section 315 of the Indian Penal Code defines infanticide as infanticide in a group of 0–1 years. The code uses this definition to distinguish between infanticide and many other crimes against children, such as mythology and murder.

Some infanticide publications use a legal definition. Others, such as the collaborators of Renu Dube, Reena Dube and Rashmi Bhatnagar, who describe themselves as "postcolonial female fans", find a wide range of infanticide, using it from child murder to female genital mutilation at unspecified years. Barbara Miller, a biologist, "for simplicity" used the term to refer to all the harmless deaths of children between the ages of 15-16, traditionally considered the years when childhood ends in rural India. He notes that the act of killing infants can be "direct", such as physical assault, or taking the form of "action" through actions such as neglect and hunger. Neonaticide, the death of a baby within 24 hours of birth, is sometimes considered a separate study

COLONIAL PERIOD

Causation

The British people of India first became aware of the practice of killing female children in 1789, during the period of the Company Law. It was noted among members of the Rajput family by Jonathan Duncan, then a resident of the Company in Jaunpur in the region now north of Uttar Pradesh. Later, in 1817, officials noted that the practice was so entrenched that there were Jadeja Rajputs songs in Gujarat when there were no female children in the family. In the middle of the 19th century, a magistrate living in the northwest of the country stated that for a few centuries no daughter had ever been raised in the Rajahs of Mynpoorie castles and that was after the intervention of the Regional Collector. in 1845 did the ruler of Rajput save the daughter alive. The British have identified other high-profile communities such as workers in the north, west and inland; these include Ahirs, Bedis, Gurjar, Jats, Khatris, Lewa Kanbis, Mohyal Brahmin and Patidars.

According to Marvin Harris, another anthropologist and among the first proponents of cultural materialism, this legal killing of children took place only between the Rajputs and other top groups of landowners and heroes. The reason was mainly economic, lying in the desire not to divide the land and wealth between many heirs and to avoid paying bribes. Sisters and daughters would marry men of the same status and thus challenge the combination of wealth and power, while concubines and their children would not and thus be allowed to live. He also said that the need for heroes in pre-industrial societies meant that women's children were not respected, and the combination of war casualties and the killing of children served as a necessary way to control the population.

Sociobiologists have a different theory than Harris. Indeed, his theory and interest in the subject of infanticide stems from his general opposition to the socialist view of reproductive responsibility. According to this coercive theory, based on the 19th century theory of evolution-based definitions and its evolutionary basis, the biological differences between men and women meant that more children could be acquired among others with support. male offspring, its fecundity naturally was very large: the line would spread and grow very large. Harris believes this is a lie because the elite had enough wealth to feed both male and female children. Thus, Harris and others, such as William Divale, view female genital mutilation as a way to limit population growth, while sociologists like Mildred Dickemann view the same practice as a means of increasing it.

Another anthropologist, Kristen Hawkes, has both criticized the theory. On the other hand, arguing with Harris, he says that both of them 'quickest way to get more heroic men would be to have more women give birth to children and that having more women in the area would increase the chances of marrying other tribes. Contrary to the theory of fertility, he points out that the affluence of some rich people like those in northern India who want to increase fertility is that poor people may want to reduce and thus in theory should be killing male children, which they seem to have done.

Reliability of colonial reports on child murder

There is no gender balance data in India before the colonial period. Since the British people relied on high-quality local communities for tax collection and law enforcement, the authorities were initially reluctant to look too deep into their private affairs, such as the practice of infanticide. Although this changed in the 1830s, doubts resurfaced after the tragic events of the Indian Revolution of 1857, which led to the domination of the East India Company by British Raj. In 1857, John Cave Browne, a clergyman serving in the Presidency of Bengal, reported to Major Goldney that speculation that the practice of killing female children among the Jats in the Punjab province stemmed from "Malthusian intent." [18] In the state of Gujarat, the first cited examples of gender inequality between the Lewa Patidars and the Kanbis dates back to 1847. These archives have been questioned by modern scholars, as seen from afar and those who made the recordings did not meet with their subjects to understand the social, economic, and cultural issues they faced that might influence their actions. Browne documented his assumptions about the assassination of female children using the "they tell" rumor. Bernard Cohn states that British citizens in India always avoided accusing an individual or family of killing children as it was difficult to present evidence in court, despite speculation that all ethnic groups or civil society organizations were killing female children. "Thus the infanticide of women became a 'mathematical crime'" during Indian colonial rule,

In addition to numerous reports and correspondence regarding the murder of children from colonial authorities, there were also letters from Christian missionaries. Many of these missionaries were also foreign scholars who wrote on Indian ethnography during their time there. Many missionaries despised India and its culture, describing it as ignorant and corrupt. Many scholars have questioned the historical record of the killing of female children in India, as reported by people who despised Indian culture, and the killing of female children is one of the reasons for their racist views. Many have realized that the rate of infanticide of women was no different in India than in parts of Europe during the 18th and 19th centuries. Some Christian missionaries of the late 19th century, writes Daniel Gray, erroneously believed that the killing of female children was authorized by the Hindu and Islamic scriptures, and that Christianity "had for hundreds of years after the conquest."

location and direct method

Miller's review of the scholarship has shown that the majority of female genital mutilation in India during colonial times took place in the northwest, and that it was widespread although not all groups practiced the practice. David Arnold, a member of the subaltern study group who has used many sources at the time, says a variety of infants were used, including those with a good reputation including opium poisoning, strangulation and choking.

Toxic substances such as plumbago rosea root and arsenic were used for abortion, and the latter were also used as an aphrodisiac and to treat male impotence. The act of killing children directly among the Rajputs was usually perpetrated by women, usually the mother herself or the nurse. Poison management, in any case, was a form of murder particularly related to women; Arnold describes it as "usually murder by a lawyer", the man comes out of the ceremony and thus is able to declare himself innocent.

The passage of the Female Infanticide Prevention Act, 1870 made the practice illegal in the British Indian provinces of Punjab and the North West provinces. The Governor-General of India had the authority to extend the Act to other provinces at his discretion.

impact of famines on infacticides

A severe famine occurred in India every five to eight years in the 19th and early 20th centuries, which led to millions starving to death. As was the case in China, these incidents marked the beginning of infanticide: parents starving to death could kill a poor baby, sell a child to buy food for the whole family, or beg people to take them for free and feed them. Gupta and Shuzhou point out that extreme hunger and historical events associated with poverty have contributed to historically gender inequalities, and have had profound cultural implications for girls and regional attitudes about female child mortality.

impact of economic policies on infacticides

According to Mara Hvistendahl, documents left by colonial authorities following India's independence showed a direct link between East India Company's tax policies and an increase in the number of murders of female children.

Regional and religious statistics

India's census from 1881 to 1941 recorded a variable rate when the number of men exceeded the number of women. Gender differences were particularly high in the northern and western regions of India, with the total gender ratio - 100 per 100 males - between 110.2 and 113.7 in the north over a 60-year period, with 105.8 to 109.8 males per 100 women western India for all ages. Visaria states that the shortage of women among Muslims was significantly higher, near Sikhs only. The Southern India region has been different in reporting overweight women as a whole, experts say in part to male emigration and regional matriarchy practice.

Complete gender ratios, as well as transgender men, in various regions were very high among the Muslim population in India from 1881 to 1941, and the gender ratio of each region corresponded to the Muslim population, with the exception of the eastern Indian state where the overall gender ratio was lower. of Muslims in the community. If the regions that are now part of modern Pakistan are excluded (Baluchistan, North West Frontier, Sind for example), Visaria states that regional gender equals and the whole of India during the 1881-1941 period are favorable for women, a small gap between men and women.

MODERN DATA AND STATISTICS

Infant homicide in India, and elsewhere in the world, is a difficult issue to access properly because reliable data is not available. Scrimshaw argues that not only are cases of infidelity known to infants significant, the differential treatment between male infants and infants is even more ambiguous data. Reliable infanticide data for women is not available. Its frequency, as well as that of gender-specific abortions, is indirectly measured in the observed high birth rate; that is, the average for boys and girls at birth or newborns from 0–1, or the average age of a child in the 0–6 age group. The natural dose is thought to be 106, or somewhere between 103 and 107, and any number above or below this range is considered to suggest a combination of female or male therapies respectively.

Higher sex rates than India have been reported over the past 20 years in China, Pakistan, Vietnam, Azerbaijan, Armenia, Georgia and other Southeast European countries, and in part are said to be responsible for infanticide, among other factors. There is an ongoing debate over the cause of high sex rates in the 0–1 and 0–6 age groups in India. Suggested reasons for high birth rate gender include the killing of women of the region using amniocentesis regardless of income or poverty due to patrilineal culture, low birth rate of women, small family size and preferred family size. once a male is born.

Sheetal Ranjan reports that the total number of infant and female infanticide reported in India was 139 in 1995, 86 in 2005 and 111 in 2010; The 2010 National Crime Records Bureau provides statistics 100. Experts say that the killing of children is a rare crime.

Reports of regional cases of infanticide have appeared in the media, such as those in Usilampatti south of Tamil Nadu.

One of the main reasons for the increase in female child mortality is associated with the proliferation of private Ultrasound Scanning institutions that often refer to the sex of the child, and as they become more accessible and affordable people who can historically find child sex. , they have started to get it and it often leads to abortion when there is a baby girl.

REASONS

Extreme poverty and inability to pay for child rearing is one of the reasons given for infanticide in India.

The lobola program in India is another reason given for the murder of female children. Although India has taken steps to end the practice of bribery, the practice continues, and in poor families in rural areas the murder of female children and abortions based on fear of not being able to pay the proper dowry and social exclusion.

Other major reasons given for infanticide, both women and men, include unwanted babies, such as those obtained after rape, children born to poor families, and those born to unwed mothers who have no reliable, safe and affordable birth control. Relationship difficulties, low income, lack of support associated with mental illness such as postpartum depression have also been reported as reasons for the murder of female children in India.

Elaine Rose in 1999 reported that the high mortality rate of women is related to poverty, infrastructure and ways to support your family, and that there has been an increase in the chances of a girl surviving a boy's chances of survival due to favorable rains. each year and the resulting ability to irrigate farms in rural India.

Ian Darnton-Hill et al. it means that the effects of malnutrition, especially micronutrient and vitamin deficiencies, are sexually dependent, and have a detrimental effect on female mortality.

THE WORLD'S RESPONSE

In 1991 the Girl Child Protection Scheme was launched. This serves as a long-term financial stimulus, in which rural households must meet certain obligations such as maternal sterilization. Once the obligations are met, the state has set aside ? 2000 in the state coffers. The fund, which should grow to ? 10,000, is issued to a daughter at the age of 20: she can use it to get married or pursue higher education.

In 1992 the Government of India launched the "baby cradle scheme". This allows families to anonymously donate their child for adoption without following legal process. The program has been praised for potentially saving the lives of thousands of baby girls but has also been criticized by human rights groups, which say the program promotes child abandonment and strengthens the status quo among women. The program, which was piloted in Tamil Nadu, saw bags placed outside health facilities run by the government. The Prime Minister of Tamil Nadu added another motive, giving families with more than one daughter. A total of 136 girls were adopted for the first four years of the program. In 2000, 1,218 cases of female genital mutilation were reported, and the program was considered a failure and abandoned. It was reinstated the following year.

The 2011 census data showed a significant decline in the child sex ratio (CSR). Terrified by the decline, the Indian government launched the Beti Bachao program, Beti Padhao (BBBP). The program is aimed at preventing sexual discrimination and ensuring the survival, protection and education of girls.

INTERNATIONAL RESPONSE

The Geneva Center for the Democratic Control of Armed Forces (DCAF) wrote in its 2005 report, Women in an Insecure World, that during declining military casualties, "secret genocide" was perpetrated against women. [71] According to DCAF, the shortage of women who have died as a result of gender issues is at the same level as the estimated 191 million deaths in all conflicts in the 20th century. [72] In 2012, the documentary It's a Girl: The Three Deadliest Words in the World was released. This focuses on infanticide in China and India.

In 1991 Elisabeth Bumiller wrote May You be the Mother of a Hundred Sons: A Journey Among the Women of India on the subject of infanticide. In the chapter on female genital mutilation, entitled No More Little Girls, he stated that the common cause of this practice "is not the wild beast's action in pagan society but the final act of poor, illiterate women who are forced to do what they think. it was best for them and their families. "

Gift of A Girl Female Infanticide is a 1998 film that explores the growing number of female child murders in southern India, as well as steps taken to help end the practice. The documentary won an award from the Association for Asian Studies

Author's Biography

I Kumari Muskan is a first generation lawyer from my family and I am pursuing BALLB from Sai Nath University and while writing this article I was 2nd year law student and I would frankly say that the inspiration of writing come to me from my teacher and genuinely he helped me very much. Nextly coming to me and my background my father is Bsf retired and now he is a business man and my mother is a house wife and I have one elder brother who is also pursuing law and if I come to my studies. I would say that my secondary and higher secondary education is not so much good but after starting the study in law I could say that it would be the best profession for me and I can do best in future. I genuienly want to thank to my parents who always supported me and trusted me and I also want to thanks my friend who had also supported me in path way. Thanks for being in my life.

LIFE AS A TRANSGENDER IN THE SOCIETY AND CHANGES INTRODUCED BY TRANSGENDER ACT (2019)

Author: Nidhi Gausai, III Year of LL.B from Galgotias University, Greater Noida (U.P).

A girl is always compared to an angel.......
A boy is always compared to a bold
Character......
Then why not a transgender can be called
As an angelic bold person...!!
- Thasleem Rayeesha.

WHO ARE TRANSGENDER?

Transgender are the people in the society whose gender does not match with the gender assigned to them at birth. Basically transgender is the person who is born as one gender but identifies themselves as a different one based upon the way they feel. Transgender includes trans- men and trans-women with an intersex variation. (Intersex variation refer to the variation in the sexual characteristics, external genetics, or hormones from the standard characteristics of male and female). In our Indian society, they are known as hijra, kinnara, chhakka.

An LGBT group is referred to as the 'lesbian, gay, bisexual, transgender and queer community' which includes those with gender dysphoria and different sexual orientations. Lesbian and gay people have been accepted in many parts of the world ad have also got their rights, but transgender is still without rights.

PROBLEM FACED BY TRANSGENDER

Transgender people have suffered from a lot of problems in their daily life which are lack of education and employment opportunities, sexual harassment, sexual discrimination, public humiliation.

While the visibility of transgender people is increasing in popular cultures and daily life, they still face severe discrimination, stigma and systemic inequality. Some of the specific issues faced by the transgender community like STI and HIV AIDS problem the term MSM stands for men who have sex with men. Because of this, transgender is likely to have problems like STI and HIV AIDS. Most of the transgender belong to lower socioeconomic status and have low literacy levels. There are not sufficient health care services for transgender in society.

FAMILIES REACTION

Most of the families does not accept their own child if he\she behave in an inappropriate to the excepted gender role and the family member start threatening to them they assault their own child for behaving or dressing like to their opposite gender. That's the big reason most of them left their own house and live with the group of other transgender because they are scared, threaten, abused by their own family member and sometimes also they are forced by society to live with the transgender group. They even don't get the love and affection from their parents and most of the time they start hating their family.

CONSTITUTIONAL RIGHTS FOR TRANSGENDERS

Right to equality (Article 14)

The constitution of India provides the right to equality to all its citizens which defines every person to have equal status before the law and have equal protection of the law within the territory of India. The word any person here means every individual so a transgender in India is included within the word 'any person' and given equal status to every cis-gender in India. Transgender cannot be discriminated on the ground of the non-application of any laws within the nation by reason of their differences and dividing them in different them based on any arbitrary class.

So the transgender community falls within the purview of the constitution of India and thereby they are entitled to all the rights as guaranteed under the same.

Right against exploitation (Article 23)

Various human acts such as human trafficking and beggary are declared as an offence and punishable according to law. Article 23 of the Indian constitution should be read with broad-spectrum as it forbids any form of discrimination. The main aim of this provision is to secure the independence of individual identity by preventing exploitation. Due to some economic status, transgender are exploited and tend to indulge in immoral activities such as prosecution

And they are seen as taboo by society.

Right of fundamental freedom (Article 19)

All the basic values of privacy, self-identity, autonomy and personal integrity are the basic and fundamental rights that are guaranteed to the member of the transgender community under article (19) (1) (a) of the constitution of India and the state is bound to protect as well as recognized the rights of the citizen.10

Right to life-(Article 21)

The transgender community must have a right to dignity life as assured in Article 21 of the Indian constitution. Recognition of gender identity provides the recognition of their right to dignity and non-recognized violates the same, they have full right to express and live their life without fear. Also, the right to reputation extends to their protection. Transgender in our society have not been seen with respect, they are often humiliated and beaten up by the authorities in power their reputation in society has degraded and their significance in society has deteriorated.

NATIONAL LEGAL SERVICES AUTHORITY JUDGEMENT

National Legal Services Authority V.s Union of India AIR 2014 SC 1863.

Judgment - given by 2 judge bench JUSTICES K.S PANICKER RADHAKRISHAN and JUSTICES ARJUN KUMAR SIKRI.

FACTS

NALSA was the primary petition filed by (POOJA MATA NASIR KAUR JI) women welfare society a NGO. The case was filed for providing legal recognition of these people who fall outside the male/ female gender binary, and recognize them as "third gender".

ISSUES

In this case, the court has to decide whether a person who falls outside the male/ female binary can be legally recognized as a "third gender" person. It deliberated on whether disregarding non-binary gender identity is a breach of the fundamental right guaranteed by the constitution of India. The case referred to an expert committee to solve the issues relating to transgender and the committee was constituted under the direction of the ministry of social justice and empowerment. This committee is constituted for the development of NALSA judgment.

This case provides us with a landmark judgment where the Supreme Court legally recognized "transgender as a third gender" and for the first time court discussed gender identity in his judgment. The court recognized third gender people are entitled to fundamental rights under the constitution and international law. The further court directed the state government to develop mechanisms to realize the right of transgender persons.

JUDGMENT

SUPREME COURT DEFINE THIRD GENDER

In this leading case supreme first time in his judgment defines the third gender. In the case, the court clarified that gender identity did not refer to biological characteristics but rather referred to it as "an innate perception of one's gender person should be subjective to any medical examination or biological test which would invade their right to privacy.

The court also upheld the right of all peoples to self identify their gender. Further, it declared that transgender can legally identify as "third gender".

<u>FUNDAMENTAL RIGHT</u>

In the case, the court interpreted 'dignity' given under Article 21 of the Indian constitution to include Diversity in self-expression, which allowed a person to lead a dignified life. It placed one's gender identity within the framework of the fundamental right to dignity under article 21.

Further, the court explain that the right to equality Article 14 and freedom of expression Article 19 was framed in the gender-neutral term. So the right to equality and freedom of expression would extend to transgender persons.

In this leading case, the court drew attention to the fact that transgender people are subject to "extreme discrimination" in our society which is a violation of their fundamental right to equality. The further court describes it includes the right to express one's gender "through dress, words, action or behaviour" under the ambit of freedom of expression.

Court described that discrimination on the ground of sex is explicitly prohibited under Articles 15 and 16. Court held that sex here does not only refer to biological attributes but also includes gender-based on one's self-perception. The court declared that discrimination on the ground of sex is also included on the basis of gender identity.

Thus, the court held that transgender persons were entitled to fundamental rights under Articles 14,15,16,19(1)(a) and 21 of the constitution. Further, the court also referred to core international human rights treaties and the Yogyakarta Principles to recognized transgender persons' human rights.

SUPREME COURT DIRECTION

The court had directed the Centre and state government to grant legal recognition of gender identity whether it be male, female or third gender:

Legal recognition of third gender-When the court recognized the third gender category, then the court also recognized that fundamental rights are available to the third gender in the same manner as they are available to males and females.

Legal recognition for the person transitioning within the male/ female binary- The actual procedure of recognition will happen, the court merely states that they prefer to follow the psyche of the person and use the 'psychological test' as opposed to the 'biological test'. They also declare that insisting on sex reassignment surgery as a condition for changing one's gender is illegal.

Public health and sanitation-Centre and state government have been directed to take proper measures to provide medical care to transgender people in the hospitals and also provide them separate public toilets and other facilities. Further, they have been directed to operate separate HIV measures for transgender people.

The public awareness- The apex court gave direction to the centre and state government to take steps to create public awareness so that transgender peoples feel they are also a part of our society.

Socio – economical right – The centre and state government recognized transgender as a third gender person as a socially and educationally backward class of citizens. They are entitled to take reservations in educational institutes and public enjoyment.

STRUGGLE OF TRANSGENDER PEOPLE AFTER LANDMARK JUDGMENT

After this landmark judgment, many trans-women went to a local court in her local court for changing the sex listed on her official document. As in the leading judgment, the supreme court recognized her right to identify as the gender in line with her identification and made it illegal for authorities to refuse her identification based on whether she had surgery or not. However, at this court officers insisted that they could not help her without a medical certificate of sex change. So even in NALSA's leading judgment Supreme Court recognized them as the third gender but the real situation they have to suffer from a lot of struggle for changing his or her sex listed in the official document and the main problem related to the sex change certificate.

Even after the judgment transgender identity is still not accepted, for all particular purposes they are still left as alone human being people don't even seem to see transgender people as human beings. Many times these people are beaten at their own home for being transgender, they are assaulted on the street if they go to the police station after being n police officer also criminalized them. Trans- voter and Tran sex workers are being ridiculed and harassed when they are going to vote.

The NALSA judgment was passed in April 2014 but has yet not been translated into reality. A briefing paper on the implementation of the NALSA judgment by the international commission of jurists says, the Indian central and state government still has not implemented some of the core directions set out in the judgment.

Transgender Person And Protection of Rights Bill,2016

Definition of transgender under the bill The bill defines a transgender person as one who is partly female or male; or a combination of female and male or neither female nor male. In addition, the person's gender must not match the gender assigned at birth and includes trans-men, trans-women, persons with intersex variation and genderqueers.

RIGHTS INTRODUCED BY TRANSGENDER BILL

Prohibition against discrimination

It prohibits discrimination against transgender which is related to opportunities for education, job health care and services and access to services, accommodation, transport etc. It includes that the centre and state government should to provide more scheme in this area. Because transgender is mainly faced with difficulty in this area they are not so much educated so they even don't know about government policy.

Procedure for transgender recognition

According to the bill 2016, trans-women can obtain their certificate of identity from the district magistrate, who will issue the certificate based on the recommendation of a district screening committee, comprising the Chief Medical Officer, Psychologist or Psychiatrist, and a representative of the transgender community.

Right of Residence

Under this bill, a new is made that no transgender child is separated from their parents or immediate family on the ground of being transgender. The main aim of this provision under the bill when a girl or boy behave opposite to their gender according to their choice their family member start hating them. Due to this reason, they are bound to leave their own home and when they outside they suffered from allots of problem.

Offences like compelling a transgender person to beg

Under this bill, it was clearly mentioned that if any person made a sexual abuse with any transgender or it may be physical and denial to a transgender to begin a public place. Then the person is liable for two years of imprisonment and a fine or both. This bill criminalises begging by transgender people so as to include them to undertake other sustainable vocations.

National council for transgender person-(NCT)

A national council for transgender people will be set up to advise the central government on policies, and legislation related to transgender people. The NCT will consist of representatives from ministries such as social justice and empowerment, health, minority affairs, NITI Aayog, National Human Right Commission for Women, experts from non-government organizations.

LOOPHOLE IN TRANSGENDER PERSON PROTECTION OF RIGHTS BILL, 2016

Bill is against self-identification gender expression

Under the bill, the district screening committee assent was required for getting transgender certificate which is undermined the right of self-identification as per the NAALSSA judgment.

Bill provide no reservation

The bill was silent on affirmative actions regarding Transgender and provide no reservation to them in jobs or other educational purposes.

Criminalization of begging

This bill criminalized begging however lack of employment opportunities force them for begging so the criminalization of begging is a threat to their livelihood.

The bill provides limited protection to transgender against sexual abuse

This bill provides limited protection to transgender in comparison to women if we saw the Indian penal code such cases as rape, stalking, sexual harassment, etc the law made for such activities are only for women the law is applicable when the victim is a woman. If we saw section 376 of IPC which define rape and it clearly mentions the crime against a woman but nowhere does it mention transgender.

No civil rights were recognized

The bill doesn't even give any civil rights to transgender such as the right to marriage, partnership, adoption, and property right.

The national commission, not enough

The bill recognized a national commission which was not enough because the rate of violence and hate in our society against transgender is very much. Firstly government should to established a welfare board for transgender and they also have to organize some seminar or conference in those areas where transgender lives and are aware of government policy and also the government have to make a group of people who work for providing help to this transgender and provide their helpline number to transgender so that they can contact them when they suffer from any violence.

Bar on separation from family

There was a bar on forcible separation of transgender persons from their family, except through court order. However many times these transgender are abused and hated by their family and due to this they leave their home and start living with other transgender. Rather than forcing a bar government should to aware of the people to stop hating transgender they are also human beings and part of our society.

Affirmative action

Transgender people in India faced discrimination in many areas like education, employment, health care, and housing. While the bill prohibits discrimination but not explicitly defined a clear definition of discrimination.

THE TRANSGENDER PERSON (PROTECTION OF RIGHTS) ACT, 2019

REASON FOR INTRODUCING TRANSGENDER BILL 2019

- firstly the transgender bill 2016 was introduced but the bill does not provide equal protection to transgender people they don't even mention the word transgender and the bill was failed in providing equal rights in civil law to transgender. It make a demand for a new bill which was presented as transgender bill 2019.
- According to the 2011 census, there are more than 4.80 Lakh Transgender in our- country who often faced discrimination in our society and are humiliated.
- In the year 2014 first time in the NALSA judgment Supreme Court recognized transgender as a third gender.
- Transgender Person Protection Of Right ACT,2019-

RIGHTS INTRODUCED BY TRANSGENDER ACT FOR TRANSGENDERS' RIGHT OF RESIDENCE

The activities provide a right of residence to transgender people they could reside and be included in his household. If the immediate family is unable to care for a transgender person, then the transgender may be placed in a rehabilitation centre, when the order is given by the court.

<u>EMPLOYMENT</u>

The act makes a rule that no government or private entity can discriminate against a transgender person in employment matters, including recruitment, and promotion.

<u>EDUCATION</u>

Every educational institute funded or recognized by the relevant government shall provide inclusive education, sports and recreational facilities for transgender persons, without any discrimination.

<u>HEALTH CARE</u>

The government must take steps to provide health facilities to transgender persons including separate HIV surveillance centers and sex reassignment surgeries.

<u>NATIONAL COUNCIL FOR TRANSGENDER PERSON (NCT)</u>

The act introduced the national council for transgender this council advice to the central government. The NCT will consist of a representative from the union minister of social justice (chairperson), Minister of state for social justice (vice-chairperson), secretary of the ministry of social justice, one representative from ministries including Health, Home Affairs, and

Human Resources Development. Other member includes a representative of the NITI Aayog, and the National Human Right Commission. The state government will also be represented.

CRITICISM OF THE TRANSGENDER PERSON (PROTECTION OF RIGHT ACT) 2019

The act only slightly improved version of its antecedents it has a comparatively inclusive and more eclectic definition of the term transgender and no more includes the problematic provision requiring criminalization of begging . However, there are various gaps in the bill that presents a misplaced understanding of gender and limited equalizing potential.

IDENTIFICATION OF GENDER

The act states that transgender people will have the right to self-perceived gender identity. But in the same section, it adds that transgender people must apply to the district magistrate for a certificate of identity including their gender as transgender. If a transgender person undergoes surgery to change their gender either as a male or female, a revised certificate may

be obtained. At this point, the district magistrate will examine the correctness of the medical certificate issued by a medical superintendent or chief medical officer.

LESSER PUNISHMENT FOR SEXUAL ABUSE ON TRANSGENDER PERSON

The maximum punishment given to the preparation of sexual crime against a transgender person is two-year imprisonment and fine as compared to that against any male or female person which is seven years imprisonment Harms or injures or endangers the life safety health or well-being, whether mental or physical of a transgender person or trends to do act including causing physical abuse, sexual abuse shall be punishable described in clause 18 (d) of the transgender act. The act does not define the acts that constitute sexual offences, making it complicated for transgender people to report such crimes.

AMBIGUITY ON OTHER RIGHT

The bill recognized transgender as the third gender but the bill does not clarify how the existing law will apply to transgender.

PROBLEM OF NOMENCLATURE

A more comprehensive term like LGBTQ (Lesbian, Gay, bisexual, transgender, queer) would have been more appropriate rather than focusing on the rights of transgender only.

DISCRIMINATION

The act prohibits discrimination against transgender persons in education, institution, government establishment, and while renting or purchasing property, receiving healthcare and using public services. But in a real scenario, the legislation does not explicitly define what constitutes discrimination in the context of the transgender community.

NO RESERVATION

The act does not provide any reservation to transgender people, who often come from disadvantaged backgrounds and find it hard to get mainstream jobs or quality education.

REHABILITATION CENTRE

In the act it was clearly mentioned that if the family of a transgender person is unable to take care of them, the person may be placed in a rehabilitation centre, with orders from the court, this denies their right to join other transgender communities such as the hijra community.

TRANSGENDER PERSONS (PROTECTION OF RIGHTS) RULES, 2020

The Ministry of Social Justice and Employment implemented the transgender person protection right act 2019. After the implementation of this act, a widespread protest is started in different areas of the country and different petitions were filed in the supreme court for challenging the constitutional validity of the 2019 act.

The rules recognized the identity of transgender and prohibit discrimination in the field of education, employment, healthcare, holding or disposing of property, holding public or private office and access to and using the public service and benefits.

Rule 3 described that all the applications for obtaining a certificate of identity must be submitted to the district magistrate within whose jurisdiction the transgender person resides and the application may also be made through online mode.

According to Rule 4, the district magistrate issued a certificate of identification on the basis of the application filed and the report of the psychologist given without any medical examination. The certificate of identity is given within 30 days of receipt of the duly filled application with the psychologist report.

Rule 8 in case the application is rejected the district magistrate must inform the reason for the rejection within 30 days and may review the decision on rejection based on the reply submitted by the applicant.

Rule 9 give the right to the applicant to file an appeal for the rejection of the application by the District magistrate.

Rule 10 The appropriate Government shall constitute a welfare board for the transgender person for the purpose of protecting their rights and interest and facilitating access to scheme and welfare measures framed by the government.

Rule 11 provides a mechanism for ensuring non-discrimination of transgender persons in public life including setting up a transgender protection cell.

Rule 12 The rule state that the appropriate government drafted an equal opportunity policy for transgender which provides equal opportunity by incorporating infrastructure adjustment, recruitments, employment benefits, promotion for a transgender person.

Rule 13 states the appropriate government shall ensure that every establishment must designate a complaint officer within 30 days of coming into force of the notification of the rules who will enquire into the complaint and the resolution of grievances should take place within 30 days from the day of complaint field.

CONCLUSION

Government bring so many bills every year for the upliftment of transgender in society. In the NALSA judgment supreme court decided transgender as a third gender and the transgender act 2019 also described that transgender can identify their gender in their legal document. It's only done after that they will be able to change their gender to either male or female on a government-issued certificate. The whole process to obtain the certificate totally violates the NALSA judgment because in the judgment Supreme Court clearly mentioned that transgender people have the right to self-identity and did not mandate surgery.

In India 4.80 Lakh transgender people are living but if we saw how many of them are educated about their rights it's too low. So firstly government should to organized time to time

conferences for the transgender people and tell them about their basic rights, secondly government should give them reservations in education institutes and in employment as an economical backward or educationally backward class of the society.

Author's Biography

I am Nidhi Gausai pursuing LL.B. (HONS) from Galgotias University currently I am in 6th semester. I have completed my bachelor in commerce from M.D.U University Rohtak in 2019. I am from Rewari (Haryana) and my hobbies are Reading, Dancing and playing badminton. I have written article on "Life as a transgender in the society and changes introduced by the transgender act, 2019" for publication on Brillopedia. I have completed 5 months internship with different organization and Advocates. I have also participated in the Virtual Summer School 2020 organized by IPAssisto.

CHAPTER TEN

DO HUMANS HAVE A PROPERTY RIGHT ON THEIR BODY?

Author: Panchami Khaund, IV Year, B.A, LL.B(Hons) from National Law University and Judicial Academy, Assam.

Abstract

We all are familiar with the word "Property" since we use it on a daily basis to specify many things in different contexts. However, property has been defined in a different aspect where we examine the relation between property and the human body. The law prohibits any external coercion or harm caused by an individual on anyone else's body and the person can rightfully defend their own body. However, a very pertinent issue of debate has been the existence of a property right of an individual over their own bodies. Although, there have been very many instances where different courts have given varied judgements on this matter, the conclusion of the matter has been rather vague. Even though a person might possess some sort of property rights on their own body, there have always been limitations to it since the law prohibits few instances like the buying and selling of body parts since then the human body is subjected to mere objects and might be misused in the black-marketing arena. Hence, there are varied views on the concerned question.

Keywords: - Property, body, slavery, surrogacy.

Introduction

The very word "Property" denotes the possession of a particular thing, like land, material things, etc. It refers to any living or non-living thing which can be owned. The question whether humans have a property right on their own bodies is somewhat interpretative in nature and does not have a definite answer. It is obvious to claim that we do not possess a right over someone else's body as there are various rights for the protection of one's body. In Tort and Criminal law, it clearly states that no one can cause any harm to someone else's body and has to pay for the varied consequences if they do so. Though our non-possession over someone else's body is clearly specified, whether or not we have a property right in our own body is still debatable.

The common law however, does not grant any specific laws to state that humans have a property right on their bodies. There have been many judicial pronouncements where it has been stated that our body is our property, and a few others also specify that human beings do not possess their bodies as a property.

While many instances like prostitution, surrogacy, organ donation, demonstrates the usage of the bodies of humans as their property. However, there are other instances where the possession of a body is limited. In cases of organ transplantation, slavery, bonded labour, suicides, it is specified that our control over our body is limited as these activities are prohibited by law.

Hence, the very contention here is to whether humans have property rights on their body and if at all, then if it is limited or absolute.

Although most of the liberal societies grant liberty and freedom to the people on most matters, there are still rules and restrictions on the buying and selling of human body parts in different countries. Though liberalism preaches individual liberty but a person is not allowed to sell his/her body parts. This is due to avoid the black market for the buying and selling of human body parts which transforms human being into mere objects. It is prohibited because some people might also be forced to sell their body parts and this might lead to commodification. Federal laws like The National Organ Transplant Act, forbids the buying and selling of organs for transplantation. However, the donation of body parts is allowed when a person donates his/her body part voluntarily and hence it could lead to the survival of numerous people who are in desperate need of the said organs.

The body as our Property- the differing views

Although the normal no property rule is believed which states that human beings do not have property rights in their body, Locke was of another view. John Locke has been a propounder of the natural rights theory and has put forward his view in The Two Treatises of Government. He emphasised on the individual rights of the people and stated that there should not be any government intrusion in these rights. He believed that people must preserve themselves and possess private property rights for their betterment. He stated that when people mix their labour with something that is in their natural form and add value to it and is not previously owned by someone else, and then they own that thing legitimately. For instance, if there is a barren land not having an owner and a person adds his/her labour to it, then he becomes the owner of the land.

Property rights in a dead body

Throughout the 19th and 20th century there was no recognition of a dead body as a property in the common law. The corpse was said to be a jilted object and was not owned. The dead body only had a burial right according to their customary law by their relative or nearest ones.

The common law does not specify much about the rights of a dead man, but the only right mentioned is the right to have a proper burial by a close one who can take certain authoritative decisions regarding the burial of the corpse. Pseudo- Property rights are granted in the laws of Canada where the corpse has significant burial rights. Similarly, in the United States a quasi-property right was established for the dead, where the close relatives of the corpse were compensated with damages for the trauma, they underwent due to the loss of the dead person.

The landmark case of Doodeward v Spence, the facts of case state that two stillborn Siamese twins were being preserved by a doctor for a long period of time, but, they were sold to Doodeward after the doctor's death. However, Spence, the Police Inspector seized the bodies from him. Doodeward appealed to the Court that it was his property which was being confiscated and demanded its return. The Court in this case had followed the Lockean interpretation and pronounced that since there was a mixture of labour and skill in transforming and preserving the corpse than its usual state, hence, the human body and the parts of a human body can be termed as property.

Yet in another case of R.v Kelly and R.v Lindsay, it was stated that Kelly and Lindsay got hold of 35 body parts from the Royal College of Surgeons and the very contention was whether they were charged of theft under the Theft Act 1968. The Court observed that body parts are considered to be property only when they are modified by some sort of skill or labour and in the present case the college had not added any labour to the bodies or transformed them to a different state. Since the Common Law also does not consider human bodies as a property and the absence of any alteration in the body parts was proven, the Court held that there was no property right of the college on the body parts and Kelly and Lindsay had not committed theft. However, body parts can be considered as property when there is an involvement of a skillset in its very modification. There were, however, opposition to Locke's theory, where Kant specified that human beings can never be a property because in order to be so, they need to be a thing first. But since they are not a thing, they cannot be a property.

Property in body parts which are detachable and restorable

There is a significant differentiation between the various body parts of a human being. Whereas kidney, heart, corneas, lungs are vital organs of the body and cannot be replaced. The body cannot function in the absence of these organs.

However, there are body parts like the bone marrow, hair, blood, urine, sperms, etc are different because these are detachable and regenerative. Even if these body parts are extracted from the human body, it can still function properly without posing any difficulty in the survival of the body. However, these body parts regenerate and continue to form in the human body.

The human body cannot function without organs like kidney and corneas because without a kidney the body will stop working and in the absence of corneas the body will survive but the eyes will lose its visibility, which poses a great threat to the body. In the landmark case of Moore v. Regents of the University of California, the facts stated that the surgeon had made pharmaceutical products for commercially viable purposes by extracting the cells of the plaintiff involuntarily. The plaintiff had claimed his property rights on his body cells and contented that a breach of this property right had been committed by the medical authorities for using his cells for commercial gains.

It was however, held by the Supreme Court of California that the surgeon who had developed those cells would have a proprietary interest in them and rejected the right of ownership of Moore's cells by himself as they were afraid that it would lead to the hindrance in the health care sector progression. In the first judgment, it was previously held that Moore has full right to "use, enjoy, and dispose of his spleen" and had the right of property on his body. It was held in Yearworth v North Bristol NHS Trust, it was stated that a few body parts or particles like urine, blood, hair can be termed as property stolen from the possessor but they need to specify in the case whether the particles were considered to be property or the containers. Though some American, Canadian Courts have declared certain body parts or particles as "property", certain other instances also specify that human body cannot be termed as property. However, the common law on this matter, has still not demonstrated an elaborate stance.

However, in surrogacy, a woman treats her body like a property as she rents her womb for the reproduction of someone else's baby. By doing so she earns a living and hence uses her body or body part for earning money. Though in surrogacy the body is used as a property, it is still widely accepted and legalised in different countries as it has become normality in today's liberal societies. Although a new concept, surrogacy is widely prevalent even in the Indian society. Since the human cells pose great value and this increasing trend has led to the demand of the cells by the biotechnology firms. This raises a concern that whether these body parts should be considered as "property". Property rights in the human body are a matter of concern in various other practices like posthumous reproduction.

Posthumous reproduction is the practice where reproduction is performed by the gametes of the deceased parents. It is when couples store their embryo for future reproduction, after the death of either of the parents or even both. The gametes are stored and then used for reproduction. It is generally done by the couples who want to have their own children despite the death of the other partner. In the U.K case of Human Fertilisation and Embryology Authority, ex parte Blood a couple Diane and Stephen Blood were married for four years and wanted to have their own children. However, Stephen died of meningitis on 2nd March 1995. Diane Blood wanted to have children with her husband and so she requested to take two samples of her husband's sperms while he was in coma, by electro-ejaculation.

The sperms were stored for future reproduction. However, the Human Fertilisation and Embryo Authority contended against this decision as they stated that it is unlawful to store sperms in that manner. They contended that this was against the Human Fertilisation and Embryology Act 1990, as it requires the written consent of both the parents but in the instant case there was no written consent of Stephen since he was in coma. The Court supported the decision of the Authority, as it understood Diane's claim to have children but the absence of consent was an issue. Since, she could not practice posthumous reproduction in the very jurisdiction; she decided to export the sperms overseas which needed permission from the HFEA. The Authorities however, declined to give any such directions for the export.

The Court stated that the HFEA had infringed the rights of Diane by imposing restrictions on her for the export of the sperms which are prohibited under section 59 and 60 of the Treaty of Rome. The Authority removed their directions and hence Diane Blood was allowed to have children by the posthumous method. Even if is stated that people might not be having property rights on themselves, but they do have property rights on their body parts and particles. The Nuffield Council stated that for storing human tissue, it is very necessary to get the consent from the person who is donating the tissue. It was also conferred that a tissue should be considered as an "abandoned object", which eventually results as property. The very stark reality is that human beings are prohibited by the law to buy and sell their organs, but they can donate their organs during their lifetime or even after their death. This point highlights that the human beings have 'limited' property rights on their organs.

Whether human beings have proprietary rights on their body is yet again debatable with the age-old instance of slavery. Slavery was highly practiced all over the world and even in India in the olden ages. The slaves were the people who were made to work involuntarily for other people without any remuneration for their work. They were mostly treated inhumanly and tortured and stuck to the soil. These included sexual slaves as well who were sexually molested. In this very practice, it could be traced that the body of the slave was used as a property. The slaves had to let go off their bodies as properties which were being controlled by others. This portrays that there is an absolute control of one's body as a property in slavery. Even in the Indian scenario, slavery was highly prevalent.

However, various legislations across the world prohibited and banned slavery as it was a very inhuman practice where a person had an absolute property right on another person's body and had involuntary control over it. The Indian Slavery Act, 1843 banned slavery in India. These laws stated that slavery and involuntary servitude is illegal and no person can have an absolute property right on someone else's body and as well as their own body.

Even in the case of euthanasia, many countries have prohibited it because although it is about an individual's body, a person cannot be given the authority to kill himself/herself. However, in many other countries, euthanasia is legal and the individuals are given the choice and authority to decide upon their lives, when they are severely ill. The issue of making euthanasia legal or illegal has been a matter of debate in various countries since there are often differing views related to it. Some countries believe that is valid to take their own lives in cases where they are extremely ill and have absolutely no chance of recovery, however, others are of the belief that it is not legitimate in any circumstance.

Prostitution is another practice where the body of an individual is treated like a property. In this practice, women use their body as a property to sell if off to other individuals. They earn a living through their body. Here the human body is used like an absolute property of the individual. In the Indian context, prostitution is not elaborately illegal but it is considered to be unethical by the law. Private prostitution or using their body to earn money is not illegal but pimping, the functioning of brothels and forceful prostitution is banned under the Immoral Traffic Prevention Act, 1956. Although, in prostitution the human body is used like a property, it must not be non-consensual and exploitative.

No other individual should have absolute property rights on someone else's body and hence forced prostitution is highly violative of human rights. However, prostitution, irrespective of its odds is still prevalent in India, where a human body is considered to be a property.

Conclusion

As we know, the very subject of whether human beings have property rights in their own body has various interpretations. According to Locke, humans have property rights in their body only when their labour or skill is assorted with the body or the body parts. However, his view was contradicted by the social constructivist theory, who specify that property rights cannot exist single-headedly and the government must make appropriate laws which grant just property rights to the individuals. Although it is comparatively clear that human beings do not have property rights on other's body, however, it is still a matter of differing views on whether we have property rights on our "own" body since the common law has a very demented stand on this matter.

As we have already seen that dead bodies do not enjoy any other rights than a proper burial, it is still being contested in different cases that if a dead body has been modified by skill, then it is considered as property. However, many other cases say that they are not property. Similarly, in the case of living human beings, many cases argue that humans do have a property right on their body parts and some state that they do not. By analysing all the viewpoints and the interpretations, we can summarise that human beings do have a property right on their body, but it is however limited and not absolute. The fact that humans can donate their organs but not sell them, and humans can store and use their body parts and cells but only with the informed consent of the concerned, shows that we have a limited right on our body.

However, we can hereby conclude that property rights on the human body should not be absolute as it can lead to the wrongful commodification of the human body and can turn the human species into a black market. Human beings might use the absolute property rights in a way which is substandard and might harm the living. Hence, we should have limited property rights on the human body, where we must have the basic human rights for our amelioration and necessity.

Author's Biography

I am Panchami Khaund, a 4th Year law student from the National Law University and Judicial Academy, Assam. I live in Guwahati, Assam. I'm currently specializing in Human Rights Law and Criminal Law. I have a keen interest in writing papers, articles and blogs and I also like to research. My other interests include playing the violin, reading and painting.

CHAPTER ELEVEN

AN ANALYSIS OF VEDIC/ PRE SUTRAS LEGAL SYSTEM IN ANCIENT INDIA

Author: Raju Kumar, III Year of B.A.,LL.B from Central University of South Bihar.

Co-author: Varsha Rani, III Year of B.A.,LL.B from Central University of South Bihar.

Raju Kumar

Varsha Rani

If we talk about the earlier/ primitive human civilization, the man lively stock was mainly hunting of animals or supply of animals. At that primitive time for existence of life there was conflict between the man and the animals. So there was no demand of law in society because law needs to modify conflicts between the man and the man.

As we know that the society is always tends to developing by passing of time. So as the civilization develops the man lively stock were change to agriculture and trade. With the advent of agriculture and trade, men were connected to other men and the saving of wealth starts, economy established in the society in the form of agriculture yields, trade and labor Further the theory of mine and thine developed in the society in the form of maximum benefit and minimum loss in the economy.

The society developed as in the scenario mentioned above then conflicts between man and man starts so to settle out these conflicts the law developed in the ancient India.

HARRAPAN CIVILIZATION (2000 BC -- 1750 BC)

In this civilization there is no any historical sources for evidence of legal system. It means there is no any proof of what kind of legal system or what kind of law prevails in the Harrapan civilization.

VEDIC PERIOD (1500 BC -- 600 BC)

Law exists from this Vedic period. It means the sources of law in Ancient Legal System of India starts from the Vedic period.

ANCIENT LEGAL SYSTEM

The Ancient Legal System starts from the Vedic period. The Ancient Legal System has been categorized in to three categories as per the development phase of the legal system.

1. The Vedic period or Pre Sutras Period

2. Dharma Sutras Period

3. The Smriti Period or Post Sutras Period

The Vedic Period or Pre Sutras Period

Vedas are shrutis. The Shruti means that which was heard and handed down from generation to generation verbally. The sources of the the Shrutis was believed to be divine. The collection of four Vedas, six Vedangs along with eighteen Upanishads are collectively called as Shrutis.

FOUR VEDAS

S. No Vedas Description01Rig Veda Oldest religious text in the world. It consists of 1028 hymns and is divided into 10 mandalas or books02Sama VedaIt is a collection of hymns, taken from the 8th and 9th mandalas of the rigveda and used for the purpose of singing during rituals. The origin of Indian music has been traced to it.03 Yajur Veda It presecribes the rituals for performing different sacrifice with the hymns, documenting the social and political milieu of the period.04 Atharva Veda It contains 711 hymns. It contains Charms and spells in verse, to word off evil forces and diseases.

SIX VEDANGS

Smriti is not meant for chanting. Smriti is meant for memorization. Vedangas (Veda+ Anga, Limbs of vedas) are part of Smriti literature.

S.No VedangsDiscription01Siksha (phonetics)Siksha means the teaching of the correct pronunciation of the hymns and mantras of the Vedic literature.02Kalpa (rituals canon)The kalpa contains the sacrificial practice of the Dharma Shastras03 Vyakaran (grammar)Panini is the 1st known grammarian of India. Panini wrote Ashtadhyayi, 8 chapters. Ashtadyayi- 1st book on grammar.04 Nirukta (explanation)Nirukta deals with the origin of the word.05Chandas (Vedic meter)Chandas divides the Vedic mantras in padas or verses.06Jyotisha (Astrology)Jyotisha describes the motion of sun and the moon and laid down the foundation of Vedic jyotish.

EIGHTEEN UPANISHADS

The Eighteent Upanishads are:-- Isavasya, Brahadaranyaka, Jabala, Hamsa, Paramahamsa, Subala, Mantrika, Niralamba, Trisikhibragmana, Mandalabrahman, Advayataraka, Paingala, Bhikshuka, Turiyatita, Adhyatma, Yajnavalkya, Satyayani, Tarasara

The Shrutis contains some sources of Dharma. Dharma is used as law in Vedas. There is no any actual traces of word law in Vedic period. Instead of word law the word Dharma is used. The word Dharma is used to mean justice (nyaya). The word nyaya means what is right in given circumstances, moral, religious, pious or righteous conduct, being helpful to living beings , giving charity or alms, duty, law and usage or custom having the force of law.

It is difficult to trace the word law in Vedas except the following indication. These induction are positive (vidhis) or negative (nishedas) indication. There are several Vidhis and Nishedas which formed foundation of smiriti law in sutras period. Some of such Vidhis and Nishedas in the Vedas are as follows:--

- Tell the truth
- Never hurt anyone
- Never tell untruth
- Treat your father and mother as God
- Follow Dharma
- Perform only such acts which are not forbidden. ....etc

SHABHA AND SMITI DESCRIBED IN VEDAS

SHABHA SMITIShabha was local assembly at village leval that deals with small matter. Smiti was national assembly and judicature. It deals with the large disputes and the cases which were not solved out in shabha.Shabha was a lower court Smiti was higher court to shabha and it was a national leval court Shabhavada, a legal expert person who decided the cases in shabha.King himself decided the cases in the smiti.Few members participate in the shabha Whole folk community take participate in smiti.

In ancient time the true king was regarded as who protect the Shabha and Smiti. Means the true king is the king in which period the Shabha and Smiti works in a proper smooth way without any discontinuity and hindrence.

In Vedas term used as law can be described as:--

Satya (सत्य) :-- The social law

Rta/Rit (रति) :-- The natural law/ The moral law

CONCLUSION

In earlier civilization the man mainly depends upon the hunting and supplying of animals for existence of their life so there were no need of law. As the civilization developed and the conflict between man and man arise the need of law enables the evolution of ancient legal system which starts from the Vedic period. The Ancient Legal System has been categorised in to three categories ie:- (the Vedic or Pre Sutras Period), (the Dharma Sutras Period), (the Smriti Period or Post Sutras Period). Basically this write up deals with The Vedic or Pre Sutras Period of the Ancient Legal System of India. In this period we go throuh the four Vedas, six Vedangs and the eighteent Upanishads. Mainly the word Dharma is used as a law. Shabha and Smiti are the two institutions that protect the Dharma and delivered the justice (nyaya).

Short Biography of Raju Kumar:--

My name is Raju Kumar and I am currently pursuing BALLB from Central University of South Bihar, I am 3rd year student of session (2019-24). My hobbies are like playing cricket and teaching.

Short Biography of Varsha Rani :--

My name is Varsha Rani and I am currently pursuing BALLB from Central University of South Bihar, I am 3rd year student of session (2019-24). My hobbies are read books and listen story.

CHAPTER TWELVE

THE HISTORY OF THE UNITED ARAB EMIRATES IN THE CONTEXT OF: HUMAN RIGHTS VIOLATIONS

Author: Disha Negi, IV Year of B.A.,LL.B from Delhi Metropolitan Education.

ABSTRACT

There are some basic rights provided to every individual during different circumstances, including political rights and civil liberties known as human rights. In this article, we will discuss the different human rights violations that have been occurred in UAE throughout the years. There is a lot of restriction when it comes to freedom of speech in the UAE. The article will study the cases of famous human rights activists who faced torture and physical abuse whenever they try to raise their voices against the government. In UAE, many migrant workers and laborers are treated discriminately and unfairly just to get benefits out of their work. The human rights of women were also exploited because of the domestic violence and the problem of human trafficking faced by them. Through this article, you will get to know the forced disappearance and torture that is faced by the people living in UAE.

INTRODUCTION

The United Arab Emirates is a country which is located on the eastern side of the Arabian Peninsula. The UAE consists of seven small emirates, Abu Dhabi and Dubai are two of those. Human rights violation has always been a hot topic in the United Arab Emirates. Various reports came forward which depicted how the UAE violated the basic rights of the people. The history of UAE in context to the human rights violation had been filled with endless torture, criminalization of freedom of speech and expression, exploiting the migrant workers, sexual and physical abuse against the women.

As indicated by Amnesty International, an International Human Rights Organisation, academics or human rights activists who try to raise their voice against the government or criticize the government through social media or by any other means become the target of the UAE Government. They were detained and tortured in the prisons. The concept of forced disappearance, which is the secret imprisonment, disappearance, or kidnapping of a person by the government or a political organization is very common in the UAE. The victim of forced disappearance was detained and taken to secret locations where they were tortured and physically abuse examinations.

The United Nations-State Council, which is a primary organ of the United Nations, had elected UAE under the International human rights treaties. But most of the treaties i.e., the Convention on the protection of the Rights of All Migrant Workers, the International Convention on Economic, Social, and Cultural Rights, etc were not signed by the UAE.

Let us study the different types of human rights violations that occurred in the UAE through the years.

FREEDOM OF SPEECH

When it comes to freedom of speech, there are a lot of restrictions and limitations in UAE. It is off-limit to censure public authority, government workers, police, and the illustrious family in any capacity. Any endeavor to shape a public association and dissent against any issue will be met with severe repercussions. Reprieve International distributed a report on infringement of the right to the opportunity to speak in the 'UAE'.

In 2017, Dr. Nasser bin Ghaith, a human rights activist and defender was imprisoned for 10 years on the ground of making some critical comments against the UAE government on Twitter about their rules and policies. There was no fair trial for his case, and he was taken to some unknown location where he was tortured and physically abused for months just because of the comment that he posted online.

Another report that came forward which shows the brutal practice of freedom of speech and expression in the UAE is the case of Tayseer Najjar. Tayseer Najjar belongs to the country Jordan, and he was a journalist. Later he came to Abu Dhabi to pursue his journalism work, but there he got arrested. The reason for his arrest was that in the year 2014 there was an Israeli military operation that took place in Gaza and Tayseer Najjar posted, a comment criticizing the Gulf countries during this operation. He was imprisoned for 3 years and was not allowed to make any contact with his wife and children who were in Jordan. Apart from this no legal aid was provided to him. Also, a fine of 5,00,000 Dhiram was imposed on him.

CAPITAL PUNISHMENT

Although capital punishment is legitimate in the United Arab Emirates, it is infrequently applied because the law requires an assortment of three judges to endorse capital punishment, which can be driven in case the casualty's family pardons the convict or agree to get monetary payment from the accused family. If the family gets monetary pay, the court can hold the convict for at least three years and a limit of seven years.

TORTURE FOLLOWED BY ENFORCED DISAPPEARANCE

UAE considered torture as their special weapon to bring out an involuntary confession. More than 100 Emirati change activists have been confined and tormented. Beginning around 2011, the UAE government has authorized upheld forced disappearances. Numerous unfamiliar nationals and Emirati nationals have been captured and seized by the express nation, and then the United Arab Emirates government very cleverly stated to the public that they have not captured any of them. They do this to hide their whereabouts, which puts these individuals outside the insurance of the law. As per Human Rights Watch, reports of vanishings and torment in the United Arab Emirates are very disturbing.

In 2012, Dubai police beat and killed three Britons in the wake of being captured for drug offenses. Then in 2013 the UAE President, Sheikh Khalifa Bin Zayed Al Nahyan, had a visit to the United Kingdom, and taking advantage of that visit British Prime Minister, David Cameron expressed his concern on the 2012 case and demanded the UAE President to release the captured Britons. The three people who exculpated, delivered in the year 2013 in July.

Another case that has shown forcibly disappearance by the UAE Authorities is a case of Emirati Sisters namely Asma, Al Yazzyah, and Mariam. These sisters were facing a hard time as their brother was arrested by the authority, so to wake the government regarding the same, they posted a criticizing comment. After this comment, they got arrested without any charge and were kept in jail for 3 months. This clearly shows the inhumane treatment in UAE

In November 2017, security powers captured two writers in Abu Dhabi who were covering the launch of the Louver Museum in Abu Dhabi for Swiss administrators. The columnists were kept for over 50 hours without speaking with the rest of the world. The writers were questioned for as long as nine hours all at once and blindfolded while being shipped between various areas. Cameras, PCs, hard drives, and different materials were likewise seized.

A 42-year-old man in 2019, the emirate captured by 'UAE' experts in 2015 drew media consideration for the abuse he endured while kept in the UAE. He has been in jail for quite a long time and has been exposed to outrageous torment and detachment without admittance to sufficient ventilation, sleeping pads, covers, food, or medication. The worst part of this case was that the man was suffering from a deadly disease i.e., cancer and still he was not provided with any medical treatment. The UAE Government clarified on their behalf that the man did not want any treatment but it is very evident that it was not true.

Ahmed Mansoor, the famous UAE Human Rights Activist who had been arrested by the UAE Government for posting false information on social media. He was tortured badly and his health condition got deteriorated. He pens down all the mistreatment and torture he faced during his arrest in July 2021, in a letter that was later published by a London Based News Agency. He was arrested again for the same on 7 January 2022. He is physically assaulted and treated brutally by the UAE Government.

VIOLENCE FACED BY WOMEN

Domestic violence

Domestic Violence was never taken seriously by the UAE Government as they don't have sufficient action against this type of Violence. When it comes to divorce, men can give divorce to their wife, whereas for a woman they have to first obtain a court order then only they can give divorce to their husband. There were such instances as reported by the Human Rights Watch that whenever any women complain regarding Domestic Violence, then the police authority never takes their case seriously.

Sexual assault, abuse, and sexual harassment

Justice is not provided easily to the women who are facing sexual harassment and they have to face various obstacles if they report any instance of Sexual Assault happening with them. Explaining it through a case where a woman name Alicia Gali a Brisbane woman, who came to

UAE for her work purpose, was assaulted by her three co-workers. She was drugged and harassed by them. When she reported this to the UAE police, instead of helping her they charged her for Adultery and arrested her for 8 months.

Women Migrant workers

UAE employs about 146,000 female migrant workers. This data is according to the International Labour Organization. International Governmental Organization i.e., the Human Rights Watch (HRW) published a report in 2014 where they talked to the women migrants' workers and asked them about the problems they faced. The women complained about the physical and sexual abuse they face.

Amnesty International is one of their reports stated that the women migrant workers who are from Asia and Africa and are working in UAE are not provided protection under the labor laws and are subjected to physical and sexual abuse.

Abortion

When it comes to abortion strict laws have been prevailed by the UAE Government. Women are not allowed to go through the process of Abortion as it is illegal according to Article 340 of the Penal Code. The punishment provided for this offense is imprisonment for 1one year along with a fine of up to Dh10,000. In any case, if any unmarried women visit the hospital for her miscarriage treatment, then she will be held accused of the attempt of abortion.

<u>RIGHTS OF MIGRANTS AND LABOR</u>

The migrant workers in UAE had been subjected to discrimination and they were treated unfairly to get benefits from their work. In UAE, there is a famous system under which the migrant workers work, which is known as the Kafala system. But the migrant workers and the domestic laborers opposed this system because it was considered a major threat for them. Under this system, once a migrant worker started working under an employer, then his legal status will be bound to that employer only. So, if the worker is facing any kind of exploitation from his employer, he still has to work under him. It doesn't matter if his human rights are violated or not, because neither he can change his employer nor he can file a lawsuit against him.

On 16 January 2020, a report came forward that disclose the scam performed by the exploitive employers of UAE. They were hiring the Indian migrant workers on Tourist Visa because a visit visa is considered a cheaper option than the work permits. During employment, the migrant workers, face, exploitation, and social and sexual abuse. The migrant workers fear reporting any of this exploitation to the UAE authorities or police authorities because if they do so, then their illegal status will also come forward.

HUMAN TRAFFICKING

As we all know human trafficking means an unlawful act of transporting people mainly women and children to get benefits from their work or service type in the form of forced labor or sexual exploitation. In the UAE human trafficking done for sexual exploitation has been considered a major issue. Although the UAE Government does not allow any type of human trafficking and considered it an offense, it is still considered a serious challenge to the government.

Many reports came forward which have stated the problems faced by the women who are coming from different countries like Sri Lanka, Bangladesh, and the Philippines to work under private sectors, but instead of making them work under the private sectors, they were forced to do the labor jobs. Low wages were given to them and they were subjected to physical and verbal abuse. Many reports came forward which stated that if any migrant workers try to file a complaint against the exploitation done by the employer, then the Police put pressure on them, and instead of taking any legal actions for them, they were expelled from the countries on the ground of having illegal status. Victims are not provided with any healthcare or medical facilities.

PHYSICAL ABUSE FACED BY PRISONS

On 19 July 2012, UAE has signed the Convention against Torture and Other Cruel, Inhuman or degrading Treatment or Punishment. But do they follow this convention? According to a report, the answer lies in the fact that about 75% of the prisoners had stated that they have been physically abused after their arrest.

In an interview, Osama Al Najjar, the human rights defender, and political activist stated that "he was punched and beaten repeatedly all over his face and body and threatened with electric shocks" at the time of his imprisonment. By this, we can, state that torturing their

prisoners have been a serious issue in UAE, and especially the prisoners who had raised their voice against the government get to suffer a lot.

NATIONALITY DEPRIVATION

If you have proof of your citizenship, then you can enjoy the endless and unlimited rights that have been provided to you by your state, but in case you don't have the proof then you can face some serious problems. This is a common practice in UAE. About 20,000 to about 1 lakh people who are not recognized as a citizen of the UAE has been deprived of their basic standard of living. The rights of having proper healthcare, higher education, and jobs are not provided as equally as it has been provided to the Emirati citizens.

Chinese Uyghurs who moved to the UAE following denials of basic liberties by the Beijing government have been kept, tormented, and extradited from Abu Dhabi. As the prisoners, China has asked three significant Arab nations, including the United Arab Emirates, to expel the Uighur travelers, But the UAE did not respond to the request of China.

CONCLUSION

Throughout the articles, we studied the different types of human rights violations that have been performed by the UAE over the years. Criminalization of freedom of speech and expression, sexual and physical abuse against the women. The exploitation of the migrant workers by the employers. All of this situation has shown us the dark side of UAE politics. All these human rights violations have restrained the freedom of the victim and made their situation more vulnerable. Protecting the freedom and rights of all should be the fundamental duty of the UAE, and they must take effective steps and measures to solve the problem of Human rights violations.

9 798886 298505